NOVEMBER 1965/No. 555

RESEARCH AND PUBLICATIONS

Editor-in-Chief:
ANNE WINSLOW
Associate Editor:
PATRICIA S. RAMBACH
Production Editor:
VALERIANA KALLAB
Assistant Editor:
CATHERINE G. TENG
Editorial Assistant:
MANON C. BONARD

INTERNATIONAL CONCILIATION is published five times a year (September, November, January, March, May) by the Carnegie Endowment for International Peace.

Editorial and general offices: 345 East 46th Street, New York, N. Y. 10017. European Centre: 172 Route de Ferney, Grand-Saconnex, Geneva, Switzerland.

Subscriptions should be sent to the Carnegie Endowment New York Office. Annual rate, $2.25; two years, $3.75; three years, $5.00. Regular issues, 50 cents each; General Assembly issue, $1.00. Orders for single and bulk copies should be sent to Taplinger Publishing Co., Inc., 119 West 57 Street, New York, N. Y. 10019. Reentered as second-class matter 2 November 1953 at the Post Office at New York, N.Y., under Act of 3 March 1879.

"The Political Equivalent of War"— Civilian Defense

Gene Sharp

Preface

Alternatives to war have long exercised the minds of men, but there has been little effort to build upon the foundation of experience. One area of such experience is nonviolent response to aggression and tyranny. Sporadically, more or less successfully, more or less importantly, citizens have for centuries sought through boycotts, passive resistance, strikes, and non-cooperation to oppose the armed power of authority, be it that of an aggressor or of a totalitarian regime.

The present article is one of the early contributions to the effort to order this material and appraise the implications, potentialities, and limitations of "civilian defense" (using the technique of nonviolent action) as a viable alternative to war. It raises more questions than it answers and, undoubtedly, still more remain imbedded in the unexplored matrix of experience and political realities. But, as Alastair Buchan, the Director of the Institute for Strategic Studies, has pointed out, the fact that "the older defensive strategies have become totally outmoded by technical innovations" requires "increasing attention to the indirect strategies for preserving our societies from domination of external rule." It may be that "in concepts like the non-violent defence of countries lies the key to the preservation of society."

ANNE WINSLOW *Editor-in-Chief*

November 1965

Contents

THE PROBLEM OF WAR *5*

THE NEED FOR A SUBSTITUTE *14*
A Function of War *16*
A Political Approach? *18*

**CONTROL OF POLITICAL POWER AND
CONDUCT OF OPEN STRUGGLE** *20*
Indirect Strategy *20*
Political Potentialities *24*
Technique of Nonviolent Action *29*
Political Jiu Jitsu *34*

CIVILIAN DEFENSE POLICY *42*
Civilian Defense as a Deterrent *43*
Defense of Freedom *44*
Preparations for Civilian Defense *46*
Overthrowing the Opponent *50*
Strategies of Civilian Struggle *52*
Possibility of Defeat *56*
The Tyrant Faces Impotence *57*

**THE POLICY AND THE
WORLD COMMUNITY** *61*

Cover photo courtesy of UPI.
Martin Luther King leading a protest march.

The Problem of War

It is now more than twenty years since Hiroshima and Nagasaki. In the days and years since 6 August 1945, awareness of the need to abolish war has steadily increased, both among ordinary people and among the world's rulers. Although progress has been made during these twenty years in some important areas related to international peace, the over-all danger remains, and our continued existence is still highly uncertain. The problem of war remains unsolved, and the proliferation of nuclear weapons is under way.

It is possible that the failure to abolish war may have its roots in a failure to appreciate adequately the nature of the problem itself and, therefore, the requirements for its solution. "To find an answer to a problem it is necessary to know what it is. Indeed it is as important to know the problem as to seek a solution for it."[1] This article, thus, is an attempt to define the problem. We shall try to determine what conceivably useful function war has played that might help to explain why it has not been abandoned, and to outline an alternative policy—a political equivalent of war—which might serve the same function.

William James' essay "The Moral Equivalent of War," which the title of the present article may call to mind, is frequently believed to propose an equivalent of war that is also

---
[1] Jawaharlal Nehru, *Toward Freedom* (rev.; New York: John Day Co., 1942), p. 346.

moral.[2] There is, however, only a very slight suggestion of this in his 1910 essay. He sought instead a "substitute for war's disciplinary function" as a contribution to peace, and for the preservation of such "martial virtues" as the "ideals of honor and standards of efficiency." It was Walter Lippmann eighteen years later who pointed to the inadequacy of James' analysis:

> It is not sufficient to propose an equivalent for the military virtues. It is even more important to work out an equivalent for the military methods and objectives. For the institution of war is not merely an expression of the military spirit. It is not a mere release of certain subjective impulses clamoring for expression. It is also—and, I think, primarily—one of the ways by which great human decisions are made. If that is true, then the abolition of war depends primarily upon inventing and organizing other ways of deciding those issues which have hitherto been decided by war. . . .
>
> Any real programme of peace must rest on the premise that there will be causes of dispute as long as we can foresee, that these disputes have to be decided, and that a way of deciding them must be found which is not war.[3]

This thesis rather than that of William James is the antecedent of this article and hence borrows the title of Lippmann's 1928 essay—"The Political Equivalent of War."[4]

The following analysis is based upon the assumption that the solutions to the problem of war that have been proposed so far are inadequate and give rise to some difficult questions which need to be faced candidly. Although a detailed analysis and critical examination of these solutions cannot be attempted within the scope of this article, it is possible to suggest several reasons for the inadequacy of each particular proposal. Since we are here concerned with possible solutions to the problem of war and not with measures designed merely to allay the danger of war, methods such as arms control, partial disarmament, or ways to improve the international climate will not be considered. We shall take a brief look,

---

[2] *The Moral Equivalent of War* (Cabot, Vt.: International Voluntary Service, 1960), pp. 1-12.
[3] "The Political Equivalent of War," *Atlantic Monthly*, Vol. 142 (Aug. 1928), pp. 181-182. Copyright © 1928, by The Atlantic Monthly Co., Boston, Mass.
[4] This does not imply that in other respects Lippmann's essay followed the same line of thought. He went on to advocate the development of world governmental institutions. In this article, however, such institutions are not regarded as a full functional equivalent of war.

instead, at four general approaches often presented as adequate and permanent solutions to the problem of war: removal of the "causes" of war; pacifism and its political corollary, unilateral disarmament; world government; and negotiated total disarmament. The purpose of this survey is not to deny the virtues that may inhere in them, but to indicate their shortcomings as real solutions and thus to clear the air for fresh thought about the problem of war itself and the characteristics of its resolution.

Removal of the "causes" of war. While efforts to remove conditions conducive to war are of course very necessary and desirable, they are not likely by themselves to lead to the abolition of war for three reasons. (1) At best, there would still remain the problem of how to deal with present and future conflicts, the causes of which have not been removed. (2) It may never be possible, or even desirable, to remove conflict from human society. Max Weber insisted, for example, that "conflict cannot be excluded from social life. . . . 'Peace' is nothing more than a change in the form of the conflict or in the antagonists or in the objects of the conflict, or finally in the chances of selection."[5] Conflict may help to keep human society creative[6] and free and to remove oppression and injustice, which are constant potential sources of open struggle. The important issues often at stake in international conflicts—as, for example, Mussolini's attack on Ethiopia or Hitler's ambitions with regard to Czechoslovakia—are not resolved by long-term attempts to remove future grievances. (3) The view that wars are caused by misunderstandings which can be corrected ignores the fact that understanding and even friendship do not dissolve conflicts or make unimportant the genuine issues at stake in international conflicts. Further, a fuller understanding of an opponent's intentions (as in the case of the Nazis) may even heighten the conflict and increase the chances of open struggle.

Pacifism and unilateral disarmament. Pacifism refers to various belief systems of persons and groups which refuse

---
[5] *The Methodology of the Social Sciences,* trans. and ed. Edward A. Shils and Henry A. Finch (Glencoe, Ill.: The Free Press, 1949), pp. 26-27.
[6] See Lewis Coser, *The Functions of Social Conflict* (Glencoe, Ill.: The Free Press, 1956), pp. 31, 80, and 124-125.

participation in all international or civil wars or violent revolutions, and base this refusal on a moral, ethical, or religious principle.[7] These groups call for a national application of pacifism in the form of unilateral total disarmament.[8] While this approach may serve to solve an individual's moral dilemma, it contains serious inadequacies as a proposed solution to the problem of war. Many pacifists have a strong tendency to ignore or play down the importance of genuine issues in international conflicts, especially if they involve the problem of tyranny, and to give the intentions of aggressive dictators the most optimistic interpretation.

There are, however, other motives for military aggression than provocation by the victim's military preparations. In fact, history records cases of military conquest without provocation. Nor is it true that all international conflicts can be satisfactorily resolved by negotiation and compromise. This view ignores the role of power[9] in international relations, especially of sanctions,[10] whether held in reserve or applied in crises. For example, if an acceptable agreement is not reached, negotiations are often influenced by the reserve capacity to take what is demanded or to resist forcibly such an attempt.[11] Moreover, while compromise can be useful and desirable, there are issues on which it is morally and politically dangerous.[12] The mere abandonment of military capacity would leave a country defenseless in the event of international dangers and, therefore, would be rejected even as a means to peace. Although military defense may itself be highly ineffective and destructive, a merely negative caution about what *not* to do

---

[7] See Gene Sharp, "The meanings of non-violence: a typology (revised)," *Journal of Conflict Resolution*, Vol. III, No. 1 (Mar. 1959), pp. 41-66. Note especially the discussions of non-resistance, active reconciliation, moral resistance, and nonviolent revolution.

[8] The proposals for "unilateral initiatives," or unilateral nuclear disarmament, are considered to fall within the group of preventative or ameliorative measures. Discussion of these measures lies outside the scope of this article.

[9] Political power is here defined as the total authority, influence, pressure, and coercion that may be applied to achieve the implementation of the wishes of the power holder. Thus, sanctions are usually a key element in power.

[10] A sanction is here defined as a reprisal for failure to behave in the expected or desired manner and/or action intended to produce desired behavior by the person or group on which the sanction is inflicted.

[11] For a further discussion of the difficulties of negotiations, see pp. 11-12.

[12] See Joan V. Bondurant, *Conquest of Violence: The Gandhian Philosophy of Conflict* (Princeton: Princeton Univ. Press, 1958), pp. 218-222; and Daniel Katz, "Consistent reactive participation of group members and reduction of intergroup conflict," *Journal of Conflict Resolution*, op. cit., p. 35.

in conflict situations leaves most people with no choice but to continue to support the familiar governmental military responses in which they still have some confidence.

World government. While international organizations are undoubtedly necessary and desirable, the belief that the solution to the problem of war lies in the establishment of a world government needs careful re-examination. Two broad criticisms of this approach merit special consideration. First, world government is likely to be a *consequence* of world peace and world community (and then a means to preserve and extend them) rather than a means of *achieving* world peace. Hans J. Morgenthau, who accepts the thesis that permanent international peace requires a world state, cogently points out that "a world community must antedate a world state." However, because the conditions for the community do not now exist, "a world state cannot be established under the present moral, social, and political conditions of the world."[13] Despite the urgency of the problem of war, such a process is likely to take "generations."[14] The second criticism relates to the fact that world government would involve not the abolition of military capacity, but rather the concentration of overwhelming military power in the hands of a world state.[15] This would be necessary to take that capacity away from national governments and to ensure worldwide enforcement against rebellious units.

The establishment of a world state could no more preserve peace than has the existence of nation states automatically prevented violent revolutions, civil wars, coups d'état, and guerrilla wars within their boundaries. Several decades after the establishment of its federal government, even the United States, with its exceptionally high degree of cultural, political, and historical unity, experienced an extremely bloody civil war. An incomparably greater degree of conflict exists in the world today than was the case among the thirteen American colonies, and there is no sign that present world conflicts will

---
[13] *Politics Among Nations: The Struggle for Power and Peace* (3rd ed.; New York: Alfred A. Knopf, 1960), pp. 513 and 519.

[14] See Amitai Etzioni, *The Hard Way to Peace: A New Strategy* (New York: Collier Books, 1962), pp. 112 and 173-202.

[15] See Hedley Bull, *The Control of the Arms Race: Disarmament and Arms Control in the Missile Age* (London: Weidenfeld & Nicolson for the Institute of Strategic Studies, 1961), p. 5.

be significantly reduced for many decades. But, as Morgenthau has noted, where serious conflicts exist within a society and are not muted by overriding loyalties, "the peace of such a society cannot be saved by the state, however strong."[16] The policies of a world government might face the opposition not merely of a few individuals but of whole constituent states and geographic areas bound together by regional, political, and national solidarity. The government would require the capacity to repress widespread rebellion and guerrilla warfare. Moreover, seizure or manufacture of conventional and even nuclear weapons by dissident groups would be possible. Thus, the attempt to bring diverse political and ideological groups under a single government might increase, rather than reduce, the chances of war.

The potential danger of insurgency might lead to pressures to make world government all-powerful and, combined with other pressures, could enhance the possibility of a world dictatorship. The difficulties in establishing and maintaining popular control over any government would be vastly increased on a world scale. Written constitutions would be inadequate. The tendency in federations for power to gravitate to the central government would add to the difficulties of citizen participation. Any attempt to prevent the re-establishment of autonomous military capacity would probably require extensive and very close control over individuals, raw materials, industrial capacity, constituent governments, divisional police forces, and so forth.[17] These controls could also be used for less noble purposes, particularly if one considers twentieth century developments in totalitarianism and the fact that a world state would be a prize plum for seizure by would-be dictators or totalitarian parties.

Whether in fact a world government can be the primary means for achieving peace, or whether it would genuinely serve the cause of internationalism in a conflict-filled world merits study in the light of the problems listed above. Perhaps it is *not* national sovereignty itself that threatens world peace, but the ability and willingness to use military power as an

---

[16] Op. cit., p. 509; see also Bull, op. cit., p. 36.
[17] See Arthur Waskow, *Unintended War* (Philadelphia: American Friends Service Committee, 1962).

ultimate sanction in international relations. Moreover, independence and military capacity may not necessarily be inseparable.

Negotiated universal disarmament. The proposal that war be eliminated by negotiating an agreement, or a series of agreements, among all countries to abandon their capacity to wage international war has great appeal. If such were possible, tensions and fears would diminish, and the capacity for aggression and the need for defense would be drastically reduced. There are, however, five major difficulties to the realization of this solution.

(1) The international situation is in a state of constant flux, with some countries wishing to maintain the status quo and others desiring to change it. As long as states continue to regard military capacity as the most effective ultimate sanction for preserving and changing existing relationships, it is almost impossible to obtain agreement to abandon this capacity.

(2) In negotiations for the reduction or limitation of military armaments, opposing sides almost inevitably attempt to ensure that their relative security position will not be endangered but will, preferably, be improved. The history of negotiations on arms reduction and arms limitation has demonstrated this fact.[18]

> No power is prepared to contemplate a treaty unless the situation that results from it is one in which its own military interest is firmly secured. Two facts stand persistently in the way of agreement: the inherent uncertainty as to what constitutes an equal balance between opponents, and the determination inherent in all military policy to err on the safe side.[19]

(3) Inspection has been proposed as a means of overcoming the possibility that the agreement will be violated. Although technological developments facilitate inspection, violation is still possible. It is doubtful whether worldwide inspection or even inspection limited to the superpowers could have the degree of certainty that would remove distrust and the possibility of a major violation. Even the retention of a small number of powerful weapons would create a substantial military advantage in an otherwise largely disarmed world. For example, while rocket delivery systems might be eliminated,

---
[18] See Morgenthau, op. cit., pp. 389-411.
[19] Bull, op. cit., p. 68.

less dramatic means of delivery (even in a suitcase) could be devised. Hiding some existing nuclear weapons or manufacturing new ones would also be possible with limited likelihood of detection. It is infinitely more difficult and "not remotely feasible in present circumstances" to inspect chemical and biological weapons, which can be produced in small but lethal quantities.[20]

(4) Lowering the level of military preparations may cause some reduction of international tensions, but it does not remove war. "Men do not fight because they have arms. They have arms because they deem it necessary to fight."[21] As long as confidence rests on military means as the most powerful technique of resolving international conflict, there will be strong pressures to resume preparations for war even after agreed disarmament, if acute conflicts erupt or ambitious leaders seek aggrandizement.

(5) There is also the problem of dealing with countries that violate the disarmament agreement. The purpose of the agreement is frustrated if the violation is ignored or countries simply rearm in self-defense. Economic sanctions would have little value should the violating country be relatively self-sufficient. Moreover, war against the violator would not bring about the intention of the treaty, namely, international peace. Therefore, although partial arms reduction measures may be useful in lessening tensions, there are no foolproof formulas or feasible sanctions that would make war permanently impossible.[22] Moreover, it is difficult to get governments to go beyond the point at which their military capacity for resistance, in case of attack, is seriously damaged or destroyed.

> We cannot expect that . . . the complete and voluntary elimination of national armaments will be put into effect by governments for all of whom there are issues over which they will resort to violence rather than accept defeat.[23]

The failure over the decades to abolish war by negotiation and the increased difficulties since the development of nuclear weapons should induce caution in accepting disarmament as the panacea for the problem of war.

---
20 Ibid., p. 135.
21 Morgenthau, op. cit., p. 408; see also Bull, op. cit., p. 8.
22 Bull, op. cit., pp. 101-102.
23 Ibid., p. 203.

This does not mean that continued examination of these proposals should be abandoned, but rather that the questions raised here suggest the need for skepticism in considering them as possible solutions. The idea that a permanent solution exists and needs only to be discovered is ill-founded.

> We . . . do not believe the problems of war and peace and international conflict are susceptible of any once-for-all solution. Something like eternal vigilance and determination would be required to keep peace in the world at any stage of disarmament, even total disarmament.[24]

International conflict is inevitable, and political groups or countries will continue to be tempted to impose their wishes by military means.

The future, however, is not completely hopeless. Other possible views of the nature of the problem and alternative proposals in addition to the familiar ones must be explored. A re-examination of long-established axioms about defense and peace may help in looking at the problem from a different direction. This may lead not to a "once-for-all" solution, but to a new policy susceptible of making a fundamental contribution and of serving at the same time as a means of exercising the necessary "eternal vigilance" to ensure peace and freedom.

---

[24] Thomas C. Schelling and Morton H. Halperin, *Strategy and Arms Control* (New York: Twentieth Century Fund, 1961), p. 5.

The Need for a Substitute

In seeking a solution to the problem of war, we must start with the world as it actually is and not assume that it is now the way we would like it to be. As has been indicated, military action is still believed to be the only effective ultimate sanction for dealing with extreme tyranny and especially with expansionist designs. Furthermore, present-day totalitarianism is a far more formidable opponent and a more serious problem than past forms of tyranny. Developments in technology and the use of psychological manipulation have steadily increased the potential capacity of a tyrant to implement his will, thus magnifying the difficulties of exercising any form of restraint over such regimes. Nor can one safely assume that totalitarian phenomena are occurring more rarely merely because the Nazi system has been destroyed and the Stalinist system liberalized. Totalitarian regimes are likely to reappear in one guise or another for many decades.

Almost simultaneously we have seen the emergence of total war and of totalitarianism equipped with unprecedented powers. If we are to survive and maintain our humanity, both these extreme developments in political violence must be dealt with. However, the search for a peaceful solution to international conflicts does not mean the passive acceptance of political slavery. Conflict exists—and ought to exist—between anti-democratic forces in many countries and in all parts of the world and those everywhere who believe in freedom, the dignity of the individual, political democracy, and the ways intrinsic to those principles. This conflict requires ultimately the capacity of the latter (in reserve or in action) to struggle and give sanction to further democratic principles and institutions. At a time when an effective technique of struggle is most needed, however, the concentration of military power and the nature of modern weapons have, for reasonable men, removed the traditional, ultimate sanctions of war. We are faced with a political dilemma and an apparent paradox. There is grave danger in the failure to meet such conflicts head-on, but even greater danger in handling them by the accepted means. Thus, not only is the question of war at stake today, but also the whole direction of political society. It may be that the solutions to both war and oppression are interdependent.

It is maintained that major social institutions (of which war is one) do not continue to exist without reason. They persist because they fulfill a social need that must be taken into consideration if they are to be altered or abolished. Consequently, if an institution is to be eliminated, it must be replaced with a substitute that fulfills the same function. *"Any attempt to eliminate an existing social structure without providing adequate alternative structures for fulfilling the functions previously fulfilled by the abolished organization is doomed to failure."*[25]

The term "function" has been subject to a variety of definitions both in popular usage and in social science. For the purposes of this discussion, the definition given by A. R. Radcliffe-Brown will be used: "The *function* of any recurrent activity . . . is the part it plays in the social life as a whole and therefore the contribution it makes to the maintenance of the structural continuity."[26] If one asks what is the function of a social or behavioral pattern, one really asks "what does it 'do for' people and their groups?"[27] Robert K. Merton points out that the existing social structures—patterns of action, institutions, or "means" toward a social goal—are not the only

---

[25] Robert K. Merton, *Social Theory and Social Structure* (rev.; Glencoe, Ill.: The Free Press, 1949), p. 79; see also Sharp, "The Need for a Functional Substitute for Violent Conflict," Institute for Philosophy and the History of Ideas, Univ. of Oslo, 1965. Duplicated.
[26] *Structure and Function in Primitive Society* (New York: The Free Press of Glencoe, 1963), p. 180.
[27] John W. Bennett and Melvin M. Tumin, *Social Life: Structure and Function* (New York: Alfred A. Knopf, 1949), p. 245.

possible ones. There also exist other ways of fulfilling the function served by the present structure. In contrast to the "concept of indispensable cultural forms (institutions, standardized practices, belief-systems, etc.), there is, then, the concept of *functional alternatives,* or *functional equivalents,* or *functional substitutes."* Furthermore, *"just as the same item may have multiple functions, so may the same function be diversely fulfilled by alternative items."* Functional needs in these terms are considered as "permissive, rather than determinant, of specific social structures."[28] In other words, a given function can be fulfilled by a variety of structures. "In realistic conflicts there are also possibilities of choice between various forms of contention, such choice depending similarly on an assessment of their instrumental adequacy."[29]

Eminent social theorists, especially Merton, apparently believe that these theoretical principles are applicable to all major social institutions and, therefore, may be applied to the problem of war. What follows is an attempt to do this, based on the assumption that theoretical insights are often relevant to the solution of practical problems and may at times point the way toward more fundamental solutions than would otherwise have been possible. The conclusions of such a theoretical analysis, however, need to be carefully examined and tested in terms of their practical applicability.

A Function of War

A complex and varied phenomenon such as war has served a number of functions. Some are no longer as important as they were; others continue to play a major role. One function is widely believed to be more necessary and justifiable than all the others and may, therefore, help significantly to perpetuate war. Whatever else it may have done and with whatever results, war has provided an ultimate sanction which can be held in reserve to give weight to arguments advanced in negotiations, and which can be used when other means have failed to defend a country's freedom, beliefs, and way of life. War has relieved people and governments of a sense of impotence in times of danger and given them a technique of struggle to defend

[28] Merton, op. cit., pp. 33-34.
[29] Coser, op. cit., p. 50.

and to further their objectives. Helplessness, cowardice, and submission to a felt evil have been considered the alternatives to war. Nuclear weapons are even viewed in this light. Although their use may be rejected as socially undesirable, their existence, it is believed, will deter an enemy from carrying out his threats, thus preventing the conflict from turning into a major war and endangering the nation's way of life.

None of the traditional proposals to control, replace, or abolish war has served this same function, although both collective security and an international police force have been intended to provide effective means for warding off the danger of aggression and for dealing with it should it occur. As Morgenthau has pointed out, however, it is most doubtful that in a particular situation the necessary conditions for the effective operation of collective security will in fact be present. In the absence of the prior development of a world community, an international police force capable of defending itself by its own means is not practicable.[30]

If war has been a final technique of struggle to discourage and resist international aggression, if a given social structure cannot be removed unless it is replaced with a substitute that fulfills the same function, and if the proposals for eliminating war have not provided such a substitute, then only one conclusion is possible. Such proposals for abolishing war could not possibly be successful, even under the shadow of nuclear weapons.

What is needed is a substitute means of struggle, which could be used at least as effectively as war has been used to defend freedom and a way of life against tyranny and aggression. The application of these aspects of sociological theory has thus produced a view of the nature of the problem of war that differs sharply from the assumptions about the nature of the problem underlying both the "once-for-all" solutions and most of the more limited measures that have been proposed. Is there a significant degree of validity to this analysis of the nature of the problem? Can there be developed a functional equivalent of military defense, or a political equivalent of war, that will be effective and also meet the broader political conditions and problems discussed earlier?

---
[30] See Morgenthau, op. cit., pp. 412-424.

Although this precise formulation is not usual, there has already been significant acceptance of the important elements. The arms control approach, for example, seems to be based on the assumption that the elimination of defense capacity is either impossible or undesirable under present international conditions. Morgenthau's analysis of the issues involved in disarmament is fully compatible with the above analysis, although he comes to somewhat different conclusions.

> The more thoughtful observers have realized that the solution for the problem of disarmament does not lie within disarmament itself. They have found it in security. Armaments are the result of certain psychological factors. So long as these factors persist, the resolution of nations to arm themselves will also persist, and that resolution will make disarmament impossible. The generally professed and most frequent actual motive for armaments is fear of attack; that is, a feeling of insecurity. Hence, it has been argued that what is needed is to make nations actually secure from attack by some new device and thus to give them a feeling of security. The motive force and the actual need for armaments would then disappear; for nations would find in that new device the security they had formerly sought in armaments.[31]

Consideration of the problem of war from these various perspectives has thus brought us back to Lippmann's 1928 diagnosis: there is need for a political equivalent of war.

A Political Approach?

Two factors should be kept in mind when determining whether a political equivalent of war is possible. The first is that there can be no simple, safe solution. Any course of action incurs risks and involves potentially severe difficulties because of the complexity and seriousness of the problems of war and tyranny. It is, therefore, important to make a fair comparison of alternative courses of action. The second factor is careful use of the term "defense." National defense has traditionally been identified with military defense, and, conversely, states have usually assumed that military means were effective for defense purposes. Are these assumptions necessarily correct?

It has been stated that there are psychological, sociological, and, above all, political needs for effective means of

---
[31] Ibid., p. 412.

defense against aggression, and, at the same time, that war must be removed from human society. "Every generation," Amitai Etzioni stresses, "believed its war to be just, defending values that could not otherwise be protected. . . ."[32] But, what would happen if our generation and the next could develop a political equivalent of war capable of providing the necessary protection without military armaments? Could there be a nonmilitary policy for deterring attack and, in case of attempted usurpation or occupation, for struggling actively to defend one's principles and social system? If there did exist an effective defense policy that avoided both passive submission to tyranny and the dangers of modern war, the whole international situation might be fundamentally changed. "Nothing is worth the destruction of mankind, nor would anything be worth risking it, if it were clear that there were a third alternative."[33] The question thus arises whether the answer may lie in a peaceful counterpart of war—"war without violence"—by which people can defend liberty, their way of life, and humanitarian principles when all other hopes have failed. The way to peace may not be through complete or partial disarmament but through "transarmament"—the change from one defense system to a very different defense system.[34]

This possible approach to the dual problem of war and tyranny is little known and as yet relatively undeveloped. Some of the early pleas for such a third approach have been formulated in ideological terms and have not always given sufficient weight to the complexity of the problem and to the multitude of serious difficulties that would have to be faced. However, these are not adequate reasons for dismissing such a policy without further consideration. In the light of the gravity of the threat of modern war, all reasonable proposals merit careful examination and investigation. Initially crude ideas, theories, and measures are susceptible of testing, refinement, and development into infinitely more adequate measures for dealing with the particular problem in question. This is evident in much of the history of modern social, political, scientific, and military developments. There is no reason to assume that such a development would not be possible here as well.

---
[32] Op. cit., pp. 11-12.
[33] Bull, op. cit., p. 81.
[34] The term "transarmament" was introduced by Theodor Ebert.

Control of Political Power and Conduct of Open Struggle

The assumption that only military action can be effective in resisting an opponent using military action is belied by evidences of non-military types of resistance. These have proved so powerful and effective that the will of the military-supported opponent has been thwarted, and significant concessions or major objectives have been won. Too little study has been devoted to these cases and to the means of struggle employed. Not only is our knowledge unduly limited, but, in addition, there exists serious misunderstanding about these non-military means of struggle.

Indirect Strategy

A frequent reaction to the idea that resistance without military arms could be effective against an enemy able to use military power is to dismiss the idea. It is generally assumed that resistance to a military attack must be made frontally by the same means, at the same time, and at the same place. Since non-military resistance cannot do this, the whole idea is deemed unworthy of consideration. A closer look at strategic problems of resistance, within the narrow context of military struggle, shows that it is not necessarily true that the wisest course is to resist an enemy's attack head-on, precisely because that is where he expects resistance and where he has concentrated his strength. Napoleon, for example, laid down as a basic principle that one should never "attack a position in front which you can gain by turning."[35] Similarly, B. H. Liddell Hart argues that

> throughout the ages, effective results in war have rarely been attained unless the approach has had such indirectness as to ensure the opponent's unreadiness to meet it.[36]

If even in military conflct it is not always the wisest strategy to resist and attack where the enemy has concentrated his combat strength, there is no reason to dismiss lightly another kind of indirection that would attack the enemy's power, including his military capacity, by means other than a direct matching of forces of the same type. It is very possible that if the basic principle in that indirect strategy were further developed and extended, even to a point where a nation might decide to fight not with the weapons chosen by the opponent but by different means entirely, the result of such action might be a significant increase in combat effectiveness over that possible by reliance on military weapons.

There is a need, therefore, to explore the possibility of a defense policy in which the opponent's means of military action are always confronted indirectly by quite different means of resistance and intervention; in which his power of repression is used against his own power position in a kind of political *jiu jitsu;* and in which the very sources of his power are reduced or removed, with the inevitable result that his political and military position is significantly weakened or destroyed.

The opponent's power is often assumed to be a relatively fixed entity, a kind of monolith, a "given" factor in the situation that, by and large, can only be controlled or destroyed by the threat or use of overwhelming physical might. Faced with the potential destruction of men, weapons, cities, industries, communications, and so forth, the enemy is forced to agree to an acceptable settlement. But this view of a ruler's power as a kind of stone block that can only be reduced or destroyed by blasts of explosives is extremely crude and ignores the nature of the power at the disposal of any ruler or regime.

---

35 *Napoleon's Maxims of War* (New York: James G. Gregory, 1861), Maxim XVI.
36 *Strategy* (New York: Frederick A. Praeger, 1955), p. 25.

For an intelligent study of how to control political power, it is necessary to examine the nature and roots of the phenomenon to determine whether it can be attacked at the source instead of trying merely to deal with its manifestations. The enemy's capacity to wage war must be viewed, therefore, within the context of his over-all political power, and that political power must be seen in the context of the society as a whole, with regard to the sources of that power.[37] "The notion that force is the creator of government is one of those part-truths that beget total errors."[38] It is a simple truth of fundamental political significance that power wielded by any ruler comes from sources external to the power-holder. The wielding of political power by a ruler involves the ability to direct the behavior of other people, to draw on large resources (human and material), to wield an apparatus of coercion, and to direct a bureaucracy to administer his policies. These capacities have their origin in the society itself.[39]

Political power appears to emerge from the interaction of all or several of the following sources.

(1) *Authority:* the extent of the ruler's authority among the subjects, i.e., "the quality which leads some men's judgments, decisions, and recommendations to be accepted voluntarily as right and to be implemented by others through obedience or assistance in achieving certain objectives."[40]

(2) *Human resources:* the number of persons who accept the ruler's authority, obey and cooperate with him, or offer special assistance, and the proportion of these persons among the general population.

(3) *Skills and knowledge:* the types of skills, knowledge, abilities, and similar qualities possessed by the persons accepting the ruler's authority, and the relation of these to his needs.

(4) *Intangible factors:* the psychological and ideological factors,

---

[37] See Auguste Comte, *The Positive Philosophy of Auguste Comte,* trans. Harriet Martineau (London: John Chapman, 1896), Vol. II, pp. 223-225; see also Thomas H. Green, *Lectures on the Principles of Political Obligation* (London: Longmans, Green and Co., 1895), pp. 121-141.
[38] Robert M. MacIver, *The Web of Government* (New York: Macmillan Co., 1947), p. 15.
[39] See Comte, op. cit., pp. 223-225; MacIver, op. cit., pp. 107-188; and Harold D. Lasswell, *Power and Personality* (New York: W. W. Norton and Co., 1948), p. 10.
[40] For a fuller definition, see Sharp in Adam Roberts, et al., *Civilian Defence* (London: *Peace News*, 1964), Appendix II.

such as habits and attitudes toward obedience and submission, presence or absence of a common faith and ideology, a sense of mission, and similar factors.

(5) *Material resources:* the degree to which property, natural resources, financial resources, the economic and industrial system, and the means of communication and transportation are under the control and at the disposal of the ruler.

(6) *Sanctions:* the type and extent of sanctions at the ruler's disposal, both for use against his own subjects and in conflicts with other rulers.

The degree to which these factors are present varies, but they are seldom, if ever, completely present or completely absent. Variations induce an increase or a decrease in the ruler's power.[41] A closer examination of the mainsprings of a ruler's power indicates how intimately they depend upon the obedience and cooperation of the subjects. This is true even in the case of sanctions. The very ability to inflict sanctions depends upon the obedience and cooperation of the subjects. In turn, the effectiveness of sanctions depends upon the subjects' particular pattern of submission, and whether or not their fear of sanctions is greater than their determination to resist.[41a] The ruler's power is thus not a "given" static factor but varies with the degree of acquiescence and consensus of the governed.[42] "If the state is to exist, the dominated must obey the authority claimed by the powers that be."[43] In this "two-sided relationship," it can never be assumed that the necessary degree of obedience and cooperation will occur automatically.[44] Any government's power, both domestic and

---
[41] See Introduction by Arthur Livingstone in Gaetano Mosca, *The Ruling Class* (New York: McGraw-Hill Book Co., 1939), p. xix.
[41a] See Austin, op. cit., pp. 302-306 and 457-458; Wolff, op. cit., pp. 183 and 250; and de Jouvenel, *Sovereignty: An Inquiry into the Political Good* (Chicago: Univ. of Chicago Press, 1957), pp. 32-33.
[42] See Jeremy Bentham, *A Fragment on Government and An Introduction to the Principles of Morals and Legislation* (Oxford: Basil Blackwell, 1948), pp. 84-103; Bertrand de Jouvenel, *On Power: Its Nature and the History of its Growth* (New York: Viking Press, 1949), pp. 27-28; Lasswell, op. cit., pp. 10-12 and 16; and Kurt H. Wolff, *The Sociology of Georg Simmel* (Glencoe, Ill.: The Free Press, 1950), pp. 183-186 and 250.
[43] "Politics as a Vocation," *From Max Weber: Essays in Sociology*, trans. and ed. H. H. Gerth and C. Wright Mills (New York: Oxford Univ. Press, 1946), p. 78.
[44] See Franz Neumann, "Approaches to the Study of Political Power," *Political Science Quarterly*, Vol. LXV, No. 2 (June 1950), p. 162. "No conceivable motive will certainly determine to compliance, or no conceivable motive will render obedience inevitable." John Austin, *Lectures on Jurisprudence or the Philosophy of Positive Law* (4th ed.; London: John Murray, 1873), Vol. I, p. 92.

international, therefore, "is in proportion to its ability to make itself obeyed and win from that obedience the means of action. It all turns on that obedience."[45] Prominent cases of mass disobedience, defiance, and non-cooperation are simply the more dramatic evidences of this general truth. Since the reasons for obedience are not constant and the degree of obedience varies, there is a possibility of controlling or destroying the ruler's power by deliberately withholding the necessary obedience, cooperation, and submission.

In order to achieve this, non-cooperation and disobedience must be made sufficiently widespread to achieve and maintain an effective impact, despite repression inflicted by the ruler in an effort to force resumption of the previous submission and cooperation. Once there is a willingness to accept the sanctions as the cost of disobedience for righting political wrongs, disobedience and non-cooperation are possible on a large scale. Such action then becomes politically relevant, and the ruler's will is thwarted in proportion to the number of disobedient subjects and the degree of his dependence on them.

Political Potentialities

One of the most vivid expositions of the theory that tyrants can be controlled and freedom restored if only the citizens will refuse to give them the necessary sources of power was written in the sixteenth century by the French writer Etienne de la Boëtie. If tyrants

> are given nothing, if they are not obeyed, without fighting, without striking a blow, they remain naked and undone, and do nothing further, just as the root, having no soil or food, the branch withers and dies. . . . Only be resolute not to be servile and there you are free. I don't want you to push him or shake him, but just don't support him, and you will see him like a great colossus whose base has been stolen, of his own weight sink to the ground and shatter.[46]

Machiavelli, similarly, noted the dangers for a prince of disobedience by both his agents and his ordinary subjects, especially in times of transition from a civil to an absolutist order

---

[45] De Jouvenel, op. cit., p. 27.
[46] *Discours de la Servitude Volontaire Suivi du Mémoire* (Paris: Editions Bossard, 1922), pp. 57 and 60.

of government. The prince must then depend on the uncertain goodwill of his agents (magistrates), who may refuse to assist him, or of his subjects, who may not be "of a mind to obey him amid these confusions."[47]

In the face of non-cooperation and disobedience from anything less than the total population, the ruler would inflict severe sanctions through those agents remaining faithful. The repression *may* force a resumption of submission, but not necessarily.

> If the bulk of the community were fully determined to destroy it [the government], and to brave and endure the evils through which they must pass to their object, the might of the government itself, with the might of the minority attached to it, would scarcely suffice to preserve it, or even to retard its subversion. And though it were aided by foreign governments, and therefore were more than a match for the disaffected and rebellious people, it hardly could reduce them to subjection, or constrain them to permanent obedience, in case they hated it mortally, and were prepared to resist it to the death.[48]

Machiavelli even argued that the prince "who has the public as a whole for his enemy can never make himself secure; and the greater his cruelty, the weaker does his regime become."[49] As Rousseau has observed, "it is easier to conquer than to reign."[50]

There is historical evidence that these theoretical insights are valid and that massive non-cooperation can be effective, at least in certain circumstances, in controlling rulers' political power. Jawaharlal Nehru's experiences in the Indian struggle for independence led him to the opinion that "nothing is more irritating and, in the final analysis, harmful to a Government than to have to deal with people who will not bend to its will, whatever the consequences."[51]

It is perhaps more instructive, however, to consider the conclusions of occupation officials themselves on the need to obtain and maintain the support of the populace, and the dangers posed by the withholding of that cooperation with or

---
[47] Niccolò Machiavelli, *The Prince* (London: J. M. Dent & Sons, 1944), p. 77.
[48] Austin, op. cit., p. 302.
[49] *The Discourses of Niccolò Machiavelli* (New Haven: Yale Univ. Press, 1950), Vol. I, p. 254.
[50] *Rousseau: Political Writings*, trans. and ed. Frederick Watkins (London: Thomas Nelson & Sons, 1953), p. 79.
[51] Op. cit., p. 249.

without violent resistance. In the midst of the 1930-31 civil disobedience movement in India, the British Viceroy, Lord Irwin, warned of the political power of such means of resistance.

> In my judgment and that of my Government it is a deliberate attempt to coerce established authority by mass action, and for this reason, as also because of its nature and inevitable developments, it must be regarded as unconstitutional and dangerously subversive. Mass action, even if it is intended by its promoters to be nonviolent, is nothing but the application of force under another form, and, when it has as its avowed objective the making of Government impossible, a Government is bound either to resist or abdicate. . . . So long as the Civil Disobedience Movement persists, we must fight it with all our strength.[52]

The German occupation of major sections of the Soviet Union during World War II, which was vastly different from the circumstances prevailing in India, also led certain officials and officers with the Nazi army and agencies to an appreciation of the necessity of cooperation and obedience for the maintenance of the occupation regime. Reviewing the history of the occupation, Alexander Dallin wrote:

> While the whip continued to be the rather universal attribute of German rule, there slowly matured an elementary realization that the active co-operation of the people was needed for maximum security and optimum performance. A pragmatic imperative, perceived primarily in the field, dictated a departure from the practice, if not the theory of Nazi-style colonialism.[53]

In 1942, for example, Kube, the Reich Kommissar in Byelorussia, became pursuaded that "German forces could not exercise effective control without enlisting the population."[54] A memorandum of the Propaganda Ministry in Berlin, on the basis of dispatches from Minsk, stated:

> Once one gets to the point where our awkward policy uproots the huge and heavy mass of neutrals who want to risk nothing, then one gets a popular movement that cannot be suppressed unless one has an overpowering police machine, and such a machine Germany does not possess.[55]

---
[52] *India in 1930-1931* (Calcutta: Government of India, 1932), pp. 80-81.
[53] *German Rule in Russia, 1941-1945* (London: Macmillan and Co., 1957), p. 663. Reprinted by permission of The Macmillan Co. of Canada, Ltd.
[54] As quoted in ibid., p. 218.
[55] As quoted in ibid., p. 220.

Lecturing in a General Staff training course, Captain Wilfried Strik-Strikfeldt concluded that "Germany . . . faced the choice of proceeding with or without the people: it could not succeed without them if only because such a course required a measure of force which it was incapable of marshalling."[56] In May 1943, General Harteneck wrote: "We can master the wide Russian expanse which we have conquered only with the Russians and Ukrainians who live in it, never against their will."[57] This change of views is all the more significant because it was diametrically opposite to the Nazi ideological position concerning the East Europeans, regarded as *untermenschen,* and to the earlier plans for annihilating the population in major areas of the occupied territory. Hitler's staunch supporter in Nazi-occupied Norway, Vidkun Quisling, who by this time had considerable experience in the difficulties of dealing with a defiant non-cooperating population, submitted a long report to Hitler in early 1944 which also contained the thesis that Russia could not be held without the support of the population.

Remarkably, Hitler himself admitted that "force" alone is inadequate in ruling conquered peoples. In July 1943, he noted that German policy had to be so tough in the occupied East that it would numb the population's political consciousness. However, he continued:

> Ruling the people in the conquered regions is, I might say, of course a psychological problem. One cannot rule by force alone. True, force is decisive, but it is equally important to have this psychological something which the animal trainer also needs to be master of his beast. They must be convinced that we are the victors.[58]

What happens if the subjects, despite occupation, refuse to be convinced that they are beaten? Hitler might possibly have been better prepared for this difficulty if he had paid a little attention to a rather different political leader, M. K. Gandhi, who stated nearly four and a half years earlier that

> at the back of the policy of terrorism is the assumption that terrorism if applied in a sufficient measure will produce the desired result, namely, bend the adversary to the tyrant's will.

---
[56] As quoted in ibid., p. 516.
[57] As quoted in ibid., p. 550.
[58] As quoted in ibid., p. 498.

> But supposing a people make up their mind that they will never do the tyrant's will . . .[59]

Thus, even totalitarian regimes cannot free themselves from dependency upon their subjects.

> Compliance and enforcement are interdependent; they reinforce each other, and the varying proportions in which they do so, form as it were a continuous spectrum. . . . Totalitarian power is strong only if it does not have to be used too often. If totalitarian power must be used at all times against the entire population, it is unlikely to remain powerful for long. Since totalitarian regimes require more power for dealing with their subjects than do other types of government, such regimes stand in greater need of widespread and dependable compliance habits among their people; more than that, they need to be able to count on the active support of at least significant parts of the population in case of need.[60]

This interdependence of enforcement and obedience in totalitarian systems is but one possible illustration that they are not necessarily as monolithic and omnipotent as the totalitarians themselves would like potential opponents to believe. There exist in these systems various weaknesses that reduce their efficiency, totality of control, and permanence. While further investigation is necessary before a comprehensive list can be drawn up, some of these weaknesses can be suggested.

The totalitarian ideology, if maintained in a relatively "pure" form, may interfere with political judgment and adaptability. If it adapts to new knowledge and new political events, it is likely with the passage of time to become eroded or modified. Pressures for regular allocation of resources may limit the regime's maneuverability and contribute to tendencies toward a more regular and traditional system. Subjects may cease to be enthusiastic and become apathetic or resentful, thereby altering the psychological situation within which the regime operates. The concentration of decision-making power in fewer hands, combined with the multiplication of decisions because of greater control over the society, may lead either to a greater risk of errors or to the devolution of decision-making

---

[59] For text, see M. K. Gandhi, *Non-violence in Peace and War* (Ahmedabad: Navajivan Publishing House, 1948), Vol. I, p. 174.
[60] Karl W. Deutsch, "Cracks in the Monolith: Possibilities and Patterns of Disintegration in Totalitarian Systems," in *Totalitarianism*, ed. Carl J. Friedrich (Cambridge: Harvard Univ. Press, 1954), pp. 313-315.

from the center. Intermediate layers of command may gain increasingly independent power and the capacity for collusion against the top ruling group. Inaccurate or incomplete information passed up the hierarchy to the center may lead to decisions harmful to the regime. Inefficiency or inaccuracy in the relay and interpretation of central decisions and orders to subordinate agents and to the general population may hamper their implementation. Economic problems may lead to or aggravate political difficulties. Despite outward appearances of unity, deep conflicts may exist within the regime, party, and even the top hierarchy, which may reduce efficiency and capacity for concerted action and facilitate the modification or disintegration of the system. Subordinate officials, agencies, soldiers, and the police may carry out instructions with less than complete accuracy and efficiency.

Many of these possible weaknesses are related to the general requirement of obtaining the cooperation, obedience, and assistance of the subjects. If these or similar weaknesses exist in a totalitarian system and tend in the long run to a liberalization or disintegration of the system,[61] is it possible to produce deliberately conditions in which this tendency is accentuated? Might certain types of resistance aggravate the weaknesses? Putting it a different way, can there be a means of defense against an aggressive tyrannical system, which, instead of reinforcing the system and attacking at its strongest points, strikes at the weak points and stimulates or facilitates the operation of forces, thus helping to alter the system itself? Obviously, even if such means of defense were developed, severe problems of implementation in any given crisis situation would still remain. This would not provide an easy way—without dangers and suffering—to solve the problem of war. But that is no reason for not considering such a policy.

Technique of Nonviolent Action

The technique of nonviolent action, while still relatively undeveloped in comparison with other political techniques, such as parliamentary democracy, guerrilla war, and conventional

---

[61] For a discussion, see ibid., pp. 309-331. Some of the internal conflicts within the Nazi regime are documented by Dallin, op. cit.

war, is rooted in both current theory and practice. Based on the theory that rulers are dependent on those they rule, and that persistent withholding of the necessary cooperation, obedience, and submission means an inevitable weakening and possible collapse of the regime, this technique offers the possibility of implementing the "withdrawal by the sovereign people of power from . . . legislative or executive representatives."[62] Moreover, it applies, perhaps most importantly, not only to potential domestic tyrants but also to foreign aggressors.

In his classic study of the strike, E. T. Hiller states that "co-operation produces dependence, and withholding co-operation provides each party with a means of coercion and of opposition against the other." The strike "is conflict in the form of a corporate refusal to participate." He goes on to discuss the wider characteristics of political non-cooperation, which most frequently takes the form of a "refusal to share in the prescribed institutional activities or to participate in political affairs."[63]

This is the broad technique of nonviolent action, which includes types of behavior known as nonviolent resistance, passive resistance, Satyagraha, nonviolent direct action, and a large variety of specific methods. Because there is widespread misapprehension of the nature of this technique, a detailed definition may be useful.

Nonviolent action refers to those methods of protest, resistance, and intervention without physical violence in which the members of the nonviolent group do, or refuse to do, certain things. They may commit acts of *omission*—refuse to perform acts which they usually perform, are expected by custom to perform, or are required by law or regulation to perform; or acts of *commission*—perform acts which they usually do not perform, are not expected by custom to perform, or are forbidden by law or regulation from performing; or a combination of both.

The technique has three main categories of methods. Where the group acts largely by symbolic acts of disapproval, its behavior may be called "nonviolent protest." Included in

---

[62] Green, op. cit., p. 77.
[63] *The Strike: A Study in Collective Action* (Chicago: Univ. of Chicago Press, 1928), pp. 125, 12, and 234.

this category are demonstrations of protest and moral condemnation, such as marches, parades, and vigils. Where the group acts largely by non-cooperation, its behavior may be described as "nonviolent resistance," for it is in a sense reacting to the policy and initiative of the opponent group. The many types of strikes and economic boycotts, the social boycott, and a considerable number of forms of political non-cooperation, including, for example, boycotts of political institutions, civil disobedience of "immoral" laws, and mutiny, may be grouped under this heading. Where the group acts largely by directly intervening in the situation, its action may be referred to as "nonviolent intervention." Examples of this category are sit-ins, nonviolent obstruction, nonviolent invasion, and parallel government.

Nonviolent action embraces the rejection of violence because of religious, ethical, or moral reasons, considerations of expediency or practicality, and mixed motivations of various types. The technique is *not* synonymous with pacifism.[64] The rather exaggerated claim sometimes pressed by pacifists that only they can practice nonviolent action is simply not true; in probably an overwhelming number of cases of nonviolent action, both the participants and the leadership have not been pacifists,[65] although the groups have often cooperated. This technique has nothing to do with passivity, submissiveness, and cowardice. By no means is it to be equated with verbal or purely psychological persuasion; it is a sanction and technique of struggle that involves power; it is not dependent on the assumption that man is inherently "good." As repeatedly stated, the major justification here for nonviolent action is pragmatic.

Although the opponent is usually well equipped to apply violent means of struggle, the actionists, by using nonviolent techniques, fight with quite different weapons. They use weapons with which the enemy is least equipped to cope, and which tend to maximize the actionists' own strength while disrupting and weakening the opponent's power position. Nonviolent action has been successfully practiced by "ordinary" people. Its success does not require—though it is, of course, helped by—shared standards and principles, a high degree of

---

[64] Pacifists may support or oppose the use of nonviolent action.
[65] See study by Sharp, in Roberts, et. al., op. cit., Appendix I.

community of interest, or a high degree of psychological closeness between the contending groups. Nonviolent action has been used with effectiveness against opponents with radically different outlooks and objectives from the actionists. It is as much a Western phenomenon as an Eastern one.[66]

Nonviolent action may be used to change, modify, or abolish; to defend against efforts to change, modify, or abolish established outlooks, attitudes, social patterns, customs, laws, policies, programs, or social and political structures; or for a combination of these purposes. Attitudes toward the opponent and the conflict may vary widely, ranging from a desire to change the opponent's attitudes and beliefs and a determination not to allow time to change the resisters' outlook, to a determination to thwart attempts to change policies and other factors whether or not the opponent changes his views. Moreover, "conversion" and "nonviolent coercion" may be attempted simultaneously.

There is no assumption that the opponent will not resort to violence as an irrational reaction to the challenge or as a deliberately chosen means of repression against the nonviolent actionists. Whereas it is possible for both sides to rely on nonviolent action, the technique has primarily developed as one that could be practiced against an opponent willing and able to use his police and military power to maintain or extend his position and to carry out his objectives.

There are a multitude of socially and politically significant instances of nonviolent action, some successes, some failures, and some with mixed results, but they could, if carefully studied and analyzed, shed important light on the political potentialities of nonviolent action. In many cases the nonviolent technique has been accompanied by varying amounts of violence; in others violence has been largely excluded. But they are all relevant.

In studies of war, one can learn from lost battles and unsuccessful campaigns how to avoid similar mistakes and how to increase combat effectiveness in the future. Similar studies should also be useful in this type of struggle. An overwhelming number of past instances of nonviolent action have occurred without advance preparations. Until recently, there has been

---
[66] See ibid.

almost no serious thought or study about the operation of the technique, and relatively little in the way of experience and insight has been passed on from past struggles to present and future practitioners. Even under such unfavorable circumstances, and even in a world based on the assumption of the necessity of violent struggle, nonviolent action has won significant victories and forced concessions from harsh occupation regimes and tyrants. It is reasonable, therefore, to explore whether its political applicability might be expanded.

The following list of examples illustrates the wide variation in political, cultural, and geographic conditions under which nonviolent action has occurred:

- American colonies, economic boycotts and tax refusal, 1763-76;
- Hungarian passive resistance to Austria, 1850-67;
- Belgian general strikes for broader suffrage, 1893, 1902, and 1913;
- Finnish resistance to Russian rule, major aspects, 1898-1905;
- Russian revolution, major aspects, 1905;
- Chinese anti-Japanese boycotts, 1906, 1908, 1915, and 1919;
- South Africa, Indian campaigns, 1906-14 and 1946;
- Samoan resistance to New Zealand rule, 1919-36;
- Germany, general strike and non-cooperation to Kapp *putsch*, 1920;
- Ruhr, government-sponsored passive resistance to French occupation, 1923-25;
- Indian independence movement, various campaigns;
- Danish resistance, major aspects, including 1944 Copenhagen general strike, 1940-45;
- Norwegian resistance, major aspects, 1940-45;
- Dutch resistance, major aspects, including various large strikes, 1940-45;
- South Africa, non-whites' struggles, 1952 and 1959;
- Soviet Union, political prisoners' camps, various strikes, especially in 1953 (particularly at Vorkuta);
- East German uprising, major aspects, June 1953;
- United States civil rights movement, various campaigns and demonstrations;
- Hungarian revolution, major aspects, 1956;
- Johannesburg, Pretoria, Port Elizabeth, and Bloemfontein, African bus boycotts, 1957;
- Kerala State, nonviolent resistance to elected Communist government's education policy, 1959;
- Belgian general strike, 1960-61; and
- South Vietnam, Buddhist campaign against Ngo regime, 1963.

Political Jiu Jitsu

Because of the variety of methods, issues, attitudes, objectives, types of action groups, and so forth, it is impossible to say that nonviolent action always "works" in one precise way. Within the technique various influences and forces may produce change by one of three broad mechanisms. The relative strength and power of the contending groups in such a struggle are always subject to continuous and wide variation, depending on the course of the conflict.

The methods of nonviolent protest described above, such as marches and vigils, operate largely as extensions of verbal persuasion and protest into the field of social action. Unless the opponent is so authoritarian that he prohibits demonstrations of dissent (and the use of such methods then becomes a direct challenge to his position), the impact is likely to be limited to the level of changes in attitudes and ideas. However, when the methods of non-cooperation or nonviolent resistance are utilized, the picture changes. They may contribute to changes in attitudes and ideas, but they are primarily methods of exerting pressure and wielding power. Directed toward the attainment of certain objectives, they effect the deliberate withholding of various types of cooperation which the opponent expects or demands. Whether the non-cooperation takes the form of a bus boycott, an industrial strike, a general strike, a civil disobedience campaign, or the open mutiny of soldiers, the action has the potential of seriously disrupting the social or political system, depending, of course, on the numbers involved, the importance of the withheld cooperation, and the duration of the resistance.

Two examples may serve as illustrations. The first is the Negro bus boycott in Montgomery, Alabama, in 1955. A Negro woman refused to give up her seat to a newly boarded white man and was arrested. This unleashed a general protest boycott that was nearly 100 per cent effective.

> Negroes walked, took taxis and shared rides, but stayed off the buses. . . . Negotiations failed to produce a satisfactory settlement. The use of taxis at reduced fares was prohibited. A car pool of 300 vehicles was organized. Money began to pour in, and a fleet of over 15 new station wagons was

added. . . . Negro drivers were arrested for minor, often imaginary, traffic violations. Police intimidation became common. [Houses were bombed.] A suit was filed by the Negroes in the Federal District Court, which declared the city bus segregation laws unconstitutional. The city appealed to the U.S. Supreme Court.

Meanwhile the bus protest continued, asking now an end to bus segregation. Insurance policies on the station wagons were cancelled; they were transferred to a London firm. City officials declared the car pool illegal. The same day the U.S. Supreme Court affirmed the unconstitutionality of the bus segregation laws. . . . The Court's bus integration order finally reached Montgomery on December 20th. On the first day of integration, there were no major incidents.

Then the white extremists began a reign of terror. Shots were fired at buses. A teenage girl was beaten. A pregnant Negro woman was shot in the leg. The Klan paraded again. But the Negroes' fear of them had gone. A small Negro boy warmed his hands at one of the burning crosses.

Then the homes of more leaders and several Negro churches were bombed. This turned the tide against the white supremacists. The local newspaper, several white ministers and the businessmen's association denounced the bombings.

The Negroes adhered to non-violence. More bombs exploded. Arrested whites were quickly found not guilty, but the disturbances abruptly ceased. The de-segregation proceeded smoothly, and in a few weeks transport was back to normal, with Negroes and whites sitting where they pleased on integrated buses—a compliance with the court order that would have been virtually inconceivable, without the forces set in operation by the Negroes' non-violent action.

The second example is a situation in 1953 when political prisoners in the coal mining camps at Vorkuta established strike committees.

> The central leadership was arrested and removed to Moscow; a new committee was elected . . . many prisoners remained in their barracks, refusing to work. They insisted on presenting their demands only to the commandant of all the Vorkuta camps, which they did two days later when 30,000 had joined the strike. Then the General made a long speech containing vague promises and specific threats.
>
> A week passed without decisive action; no clear orders came from Moscow. Food would continue only while existing provisions lasted, it was announced. A strike leaflet appeared in

thousands of copies urging self-reliance to gain freedom, and the strike as the only possible means of action. Sympathetic soldiers helped to spread these and to maintain contacts between the camps. Twenty big pits were shut down.

Russian-speaking troops were then withdrawn and replaced by soldiers from the Far East tribes. With the strike at its peak in early August, the State Prosecutor arrived with several generals from Moscow, offering minor concessions: two letters home a month (instead of a year), one visit a year, removal of identification numbers from clothes and of iron bars from barracks windows.

In an open letter, the strike leadership rejected these. The Prosecutor spoke at the camps, promising better food, higher pay, shorter shifts. Only a few wavered. The Strike Committee leaders went to an interview with the General, but never returned. [Some strikers were shot.]

After holding out for over three months the strike finally ended in face of food and fuel shortages. Considerable material improvements were made, and a spokesman of the International Commission on Concentration Camp Practices considered the strike action in this and other camps to have been one of the most important factors in the improvement in the lot of the political prisoners.[67]

Methods of nonviolent intervention, such as sit-ins, nonviolent raids to demand possession of certain objects or places, nonviolent occupation of specific places by multitudes of people, or parallel government operating in rivalry to the opponent's regime, are all methods that go beyond the withholding of desired or expected cooperation. They challenge the opponent's authority and capacity to rule. Although undoubtedly of more limited applicability than the methods of non-cooperation, in particular circumstances they may be used advantageously to the detriment of the opponent's authority and capacity to maintain his system. The choice of methods determines to a considerable degree how the technique will work in a given situation.

This, however, is not the only factor. It is assumed in the following discussion that while methods of nonviolent protest may be used, the bulk of the action is conducted by non-cooperation with a limited use of nonviolent intervention. If the nonviolent action is then applied at vulnerable points with appropriate numbers and maintained over an adequate period

---

[67] For text of both examples, see Sharp, *Creative Conflict in Politics* (London: Housmans, 1962), pp. 5-6.

of time (these will vary with the case), the result is likely to be a challenge to the opponent's position, policy, or power, which he may not be able to ignore as was evident, for example, in Berlin in 1943. The Gestapo carried out a massive raid, arresting every Jew in Germany. Those with "Aryan kin" were placed in a separate prison. The following day wives of the Aryan-related prisoners turned up en masse at the gate of the detention center.

> In vain the security police tried to turn away the demonstrators, some 6,000 of them, and to disperse them. Again and again they massed together, advanced, called for their husbands, who despite strict instructions to the contrary, showed themselves at the windows, and demanded their release.
> For a few hours the routine of a working day interrupted the demonstration, but in the afternoon the square was again crammed with people, and the demanding, accusing cries of the women rose above the noise of the traffic like passionate avowals of a love strengthened by the bitterness of life.
> Gestapo headquarters was situated in the Burgstrasse, not far from the square where the demonstration was taking place. A few salvoes from a machine gun could have wiped the women off the square, but the SS did not fire, not this time. Scared by an incident which had no equal in the history of the Third Reich, headquarters consented to negotiate. They spoke soothingly, gave assurances, and finally released the prisoners.[68]

The opponent may find that, if he is not to give in readily to the demands of the nonviolent actionists, he must apply sanctions against them in an effort to halt their action and obtain cooperation and submission. Exactly how severe his sanctions may be will vary with the seriousness of the nonviolent challenge, the importance of the issue at stake, the political situation, and the nature of the opponent.

Repression or other countermeasures are to be expected in most situations. This repression would probably involve the threat or use of physical violence, including imprisonment, beatings, shootings, and perhaps executions. But these means do not necessarily produce submission; nonviolent action is a technique designed to operate against opponents with the capacity for, and the willingness to, apply violence to attain their objectives. For sanctions to be effective, they must operate on

---

[68] Heinz Ullstein translation reproduced in Theodor Ebert, "Effects of repression by the invader," *Peace News* (London), 19 Mar. 1965.

the minds of the subjects and produce fear and the consequent willingness to obey. In nonviolent action, danger of injury or death does not necessarily cause the combatants to withdraw any more than it does on the battlefield. If the nonviolent actionists are willing to pay the price of resistance, the repression may not produce the desired submission. Arrests and selected reprisals may increase the spirit of resistance as they did in Nazi-occupied Norway. This, for example, was evident in the attempt to put all the teachers into a "corporation" under the head of the Norwegian Gestapo.

> The underground called on the teachers to resist by writing to Quisling's Education Department, stating they could not assist in promoting fascist education of the children nor regard themselves members of the new teachers' organization.
> Between 8,000 and 10,000 of the country's 12,000 teachers wrote such letters, each signing their names and addresses to the prescribed wording.
> After threatening dismissal, the [Quisling] Government closed all schools for a month. The teachers then held classes in private homes. Despite censorship, news of the resistance spread. Tens of thousands of letters of protest poured into the Government office from parents.
> After the deadline for compliance had passed, about 1,000 teachers were arrested and sent to concentration camps. As their cattle trucks passed through, children sang at the railway stations.
> In the camps, the Gestapo imposed an atmosphere of terror. On starvation rations, the teachers were put through "torture gymnastics" in deep snow. Only a very few gave in. When the spirit of resistance remained unaffected, the "treatment" continued.
> When the schools were re-opened, the remaining teachers told their pupils they repudiated membership in the new organization and spoke of a duty to conscience.
> Rumours were spread that if the teachers at their jobs did not give in, some or all of those arrested would meet death in one way or another. [The] teachers stood firm.
> Then, by cattle truck trains and overcrowded steamers, the arrested teachers were shipped to a camp near Kirkenes, in the Far North. . . . Their suffering strengthened the home front morale, while it posted several problems to Quisling and his followers. On one occasion, Quisling raged at the teachers of a school near Oslo, ending: "You teachers have destroyed everything for me!"

Fearful of alienating the Norwegians still further from his regime, Quisling finally ordered the teachers' release. Eight months after the arrests, the last of the teachers returned home to triumphal receptions.[69]

There is a fairly common assumption that victory inevitably comes to him who wields the greatest military power. It seems incredible that citizens without military weapons can thwart an enemy willing and able to use violence to achieve his goals. The military or paramilitary, it can be argued, are a highly professional group, responding not to their own self-imposed drives but to commands and trained reflexes. How can any citizenry turn itself, of its own volition, into a "sitting duck?" The answer is that this has happened in the past—the struggle of the Buddhist priests in South Vietnam is one of the most dramatic recent examples—and there is no reason that it cannot and will not happen again. In fact, the opponent may find that nonviolent action is more intangible and difficult to overcome than overt violence. Not only is it difficult to justify repressive violence against nonviolent people, but such violence, instead of strengthening the opponent's position and weakening the nonviolent actionists, may achieve the reverse. In short, the nonviolent technique applied against a violent opponent uses the opponent's "strength," as in *jiu jitsu,* to upset his balance and contribute to his own defeat. This is not simply because of the novelty of nonviolent action, which with the spread of the technique is already wearing off, but because of the inherent nature of the technique itself.

Violence against nonviolent citizens may also alienate the general populace from the opponent's regime. Repression may rally public opinion to the support of the nonviolent actionists (though its effectiveness varies), which may lead to supporting action. Repression may even alienate the opponent's own subjects, usual supporters, and agents; initial uneasiness may lead to internal opposition and, at times, to non-cooperation and disobedience. If the repression does lead to a significant increase in the number of nonviolent actionists, and conceivably also to action such as strikes, disobedience, and troop mutiny among the opponent's own supporters, the repression clearly will have rebounded against the regime.

---
[69] Sharp, *Creative Conflict in Politics,* op. cit., p. 3.

Furthermore, apart from this *jiu jitsu* effect, the repression may be highly ineffective in bending the actionists to the opponent's will. The arrest of the leadership may simply lead to the movement developing in such a way as to enable it to carry on, first, with secondary lines of leaders (either preselected or who have emerged from the ranks) and, possibly later, even without a recognizable leadership. The opponent may make new acts illegal only to find that he has opened up new opportunities for defiance. While he attempts to repress defiance at certain points, the nonviolent actionists may develop sufficient strength to broaden their attack on other fronts and challenge his very ability to rule. Instead of mass repression forcing cooperation and obedience, the opponent may discover that the repression is constantly being met with refusal to submit or flee. In extreme cases, the very agencies of repression may be immobilized by the massive defiance. Physically incapable of enforcing the opponent's will, the police may abandon the struggle, officials resign, and troops mutiny. This situation, it is emphasized, cannot be produced except when the aims of the nonviolent actionists have the overwhelming support of the populace and when the activists and the population are willing to pay the price. There have been situations in the past when mass defiance by the populace has made a government powerless. One vivid illustration of this is the 1920 military coup which failed to overthrow the young Weimar Republic. On 10 March, a year after the Republic had been established, the government was presented with a virtual ultimatum by General von Lüttwitz on behalf of a right-wing pro-monarchist group led by Lüttwitz and a German politician, Wolfgang Kapp. The group's demands included new elections, a cabinet of "experts," and a halt to the disbandment of the armed forces (in accordance with provisions of the Versailles Treaty). The ultimatum was rejected, and the same day the Kappists began their march on Berlin. Police officers sided with the conspirators, and the government troops could not be trusted to oppose them.

President Friedrich Ebert and his government abandoned Berlin without a fight, retreating first to Dresden and then to Stuttgart. Berlin was occupied on 13 March, and Kapp proclaimed himself Chancellor of the Reich. The Ebert Cabinet and the Executive Committee of the Social Democratic Party retaliated by calling for a general strike: "There is but one means to prevent the return of Wilhem II; the paralysis of all economic life. Not a hand must stir, not a worker give aid to the military dictatorship." Thousands had already initiated a spontaneous strike in Berlin, so that by 14 March the general strike, supported by workers of all political and religious groups, was in full swing. No "essential services" were exempted. Seizure of two pro-Ebert newspapers in Berlin led to a printers' strike. The Kappist regime lacked money, and civil servants struck or refused to head ministries under Kapp.

On 15 March, the Ebert government rejected proposals for a compromise. Leaflets titled "The Collapse of the Military Dictatorship" were showered by plane on Berlin. Some *Reichswehr* commanders defected from the Kappist regime. The strike continued to spread despite severe threats and the shooting of some strikers. On the morning of 17 March, the Berlin Security Police changed its attitude and demanded Kapp's resignation. Later that day Kapp resigned and fled to Sweden. Bloody clashes took place in many towns, but by evening most of the conspirators had left Berlin and Lüttwitz had resigned. The leaders of the coup had been defeated, and the Weimar Republic was preserved.[70]

---

[70] For more details, see Wilfrid Harris Crook, *The General Strike: A Study of Labor's Tragic Weapon in Theory and Practice* (Chapel Hill: Univ. of North Carolina Press, 1931), pp. 496-527, and D. J. Goodspeed, *The Conspirators: A Study of the Coup d'Etat* (New York: Viking Press, 1962), pp. 108-143 and 211-213.

Civilian Defense Policy

A civilian defense policy has three main characteristics. First, it is designed to be a defense policy capable of practical operation under existing political and international conditions, although it may also contribute to significant changes in international relations. Second, it is a civilian as contrasted to a military defense policy. Military attack would be met with the quite different non-military sanctions of defiance and nonviolent non-cooperation. Present military personnel would not by definition be excluded from the implementation of the policy, but military means of defense would be replaced with civilian means. Third, it is a policy to be carried out by the civilians as a whole and not conducted for them by a small group of professionals or by an organization set apart from the rest of the society, although specialists and organizations would be needed. In crises, the effectiveness of this policy would ultimately depend to a much greater degree on the active participation of the citizens themselves in the defense of their political freedom and political society than in the case of military defense.

There is almost no doubt that a civilian defense policy would have to be considered and adopted through the normal democratic process and governmental decision. The governmental apparatus and resources would then be available for the preparation of the new policy, which would have to be considerable, and for assistance during the change-over.

There are two important differences between civilian and military defense. Civilian defense is designed not only to deal with external threats to freedom by invasion, but also to defeat attempts to destroy democratic government by means of a coup d'état, with or without external encouragement and assistance. Many parliamentary regimes have been ousted by such coups. Barring civil war, however, there has been virtually no defense capacity for such contingencies if the army leads or backs the coup as has often happened. This extension of defense capacity in the new policy would help to deter both the usual types of coups d'état and possible coups by very small political extremist groups once the military establishment has been abolished. Civilian defense cannot defend geographical borders or territorial integrity as such, but as a rule neither can the military establishment. Even the superpowers cannot ensure their territories against nuclear devastation.

The purpose of civilian defense would be to make the establishment and maintenance of control over the country impossible and, at the same time, set in motion influences in the invader's own country that would be internationally harmful to his regime and to the military venture. The primary attempt to defend free social and political institutions, and the principles underlying them, would thus finally lead to a geographic withdrawal or collapse of the invader. The advantage of this approach is the probability that it would considerably reduce physical destruction and loss of life, while making it possible to refuse to surrender despite occupation.

Civilian Defense as a Deterrent

If an aggressive regime is deciding whether or not to attempt an invasion to take possession of another state, it will usually take into consideration a number of factors. These will include estimates of the relative ease or difficulty of the invasion and subsequent control of the country, and estimates of anticipated gains as compared to costs of the whole operation, including economic, political, ideological, military, and other aspects. If the prospective invasion is not based on a huge gamble or pure irrationality, the likelihood of considerably greater losses and disadvantages than gains will probably discourage or deter the invader.

It is commonly claimed that strong military defense capacity can serve as an effective deterrent by making an invasion extremely costly, reducing possibilities for success, running a very low chance of defeating it, or promising massive retaliatory destruction. There is no reason to assume, however, that military power is the only available deterrent. Invasion is not an objective in and of itself. It is seen as a way to achieve a wider purpose, which almost inevitably will involve occupation of the country. If, however, a successful invasion is to be followed by immense difficulties in occupying and controlling the invaded territory and its population, this may be at least as effective a deterrent as military capacity to combat the invasion. Such control on a large scale is a problem even in the absence of well-prepared capacity for resistance. George F. Kennan has argued the difficulties of achieving and maintaining control over large conquered areas.

> There is no magic by which great nations are brought to obey for any length of time the will of people very far away who understand their problems poorly and with whom they feel no intimacy of origin or understanding. This has to be done by bayonets, or it is not done at all.[71]

Although he is not an advocate of civilian defense and has urged continuation of the nuclear deterrent, his 1957 Reith Lectures stressed the importance of the non-military component of Western resistance to communism. "The Soviet threat," he declared, "is a combined military-political threat, with the accent on the political." He propounded a "strategic doctrine addressed to this reality." This doctrine, which included military or preferably paramilitary forces, emphasized the need to strengthen the "internal health and discipline of the respective national societies, and of the manner in which they were organized to prevent the conquest and subjugation of their national life by unscrupulous and foreign-inspired minorities in their midst." Such a strategy would not be designed primarily to defend the frontiers,

---

[71] *Russia and the West under Lenin and Stalin* (Boston: Little, Brown and Co., 1961), p. 276. Copyright © 1960, 1961 by James K. Hotchkiss, Trustee, with permission of Atlantic-Little, Brown and Co.

but rather its defense at every village crossroads. The purpose would be to place the country in a position where it could face the Kremlin and say to it: "Look here, you may be able to overrun us, if you are unwise enough to attempt it, but you will have a small profit from it; we are in a position to assure that not a single Communist or other person likely to perform your political business will be available to you for this purpose; you will find here no adequate nucleus of a puppet regime; on the contrary, you will be faced with the united and organized hostility of an entire nation; your stay among us will not be a happy one; we will make you pay bitterly for every day of it; and it will be without favorable long-term political prospects."

A country in a position to demonstrate its ability to do this would, he maintained, "have little need of foreign garrisons to assure its immunity from Soviet attack." Moreover, defense based largely on organized civil resistance "could be maintained at a fraction of the cost per unit of the present conventional establishments."[72]

Defense of Freedom

A reconsideration of policies and preparations for civilian defense would necessitate a careful examination of the principles, qualities, and institutions of the society that were deemed worthy of defense. Widespread understanding of, clarification of, and commitment to democratic principles and institutions would be an important early stage in transarmament to civilian defense.[73] But, while defense motivations and aims ought to be under regular development and consideration, there are certain minimum principles in which general agreement should be possible. The formulation that Arne Naess has offered in regard to Norwegian defense might serve, in a modified form, as the basis for a description of the defense motivations and aims of other countries.

> To defend Norway today means to defend our independence, our freedom to shape our lives within the framework of Norwegian social traditions and cultures and to change them as

---
[72] *Russia, the Atom, and the West* (New York: Harper and Bros., 1958), pp. 62-65.
[73] See Arne Naess, "Non-military defence and foreign policy," in Roberts, et al., op. cit., p. 36.

we wish. It is to defend a way of life against all external forces that would alter it without our consent.[74]

One of these basic principles in combatting attempted occupations and seizures of power is, as has been emphasized, that defense is the responsibility of the citizens themselves. Civilian defense extends the principle that the price of liberty is eternal vigilance to the strategy and specific implementation of the country's defense policy. This principle, of course, is not new. Its earlier applications are symbolized by the guns above the fireplaces in Swiss houses, the early American Minutemen, and the constitutional guarantee of the "right to bear arms." But, as Carl J. Friedrich has reiterated, technological developments, primarily in modern weaponry, have virtually destroyed this as a practical principle (except perhaps in a very indirect and abstract sense).[75] Civilian defense, by relying on a technique of struggle not dependent upon military technology, restores the role and importance of individuals in the defense of their freedom and political society. "Eternal vigilance" ceases to be a romantic slogan of an earlier age and becomes a fundamental principle on which the defense policy is built.

Preparations for Civilian Defense

There is general agreement that, although it is never easy, it is less difficult to resist a tyrannical regime while it is seeking to establish itself rather than after it has succeeded. Kennan, in reference to the seizure of power by a totalitarian regime, points to the necessity for certain states of mind and behavior among the subjects. "For the seizure of power, a certain degree of mass bewilderment and passivity are required."[76] The advanced preparations and training for a civilian defense policy are designed precisely to prevent that condition; the usurper will encounter a population prepared to fight for its freedom. Thus, subject to the adequacy of such preparations and the effective-

---

[74] Ibid., p. 34.
[75] "The Unique Character of Totalitarian Society," in *Totalitarianism*, op. cit., p. 56. "If men wish to defend themselves against a violent invader on the level of violence, it is the invader who dictates to the defender what methods of combat he shall use." Bart. de Ligt, *The Conquest of Violence: An Essay on War and Revolution* (New York: E. P. Dutton & Co., 1938), p. 198.
[76] "Totalitarianism in the Modern World," in *Totalitarianism*, op. cit., p. 23.

ness with which the struggle is conducted, the invader or internal usurper is likely to face an extraordinarily difficult task in establishing and consolidating his regime.

Adoption of a civilian defense policy would require both general and specific preparations. Since no country is likely to abandon military defense until it has confidence in and is prepared to apply an alternative defense policy, for a significant period these preparations would be carried out simultaneously with continued military measures. Because of their different natures, the two policies would probably require separate institutional arrangements; during the transitional period, personnel and money would be needed for both. Detailed consideration of the various aspects of preparations for civilian defense necessarily lies outside the scope of this article. The broad types of preparations listed here, therefore, are only suggestive of the extensive program that would have to be developed.[77]

A major educational program to introduce the nature and purpose of the new defense policy would be needed for the country as a whole. This probably could best be implemented by central, state, and local governmental bodies, assisted by various independent institutions, such as schools, churches, trade unions, and business groups. People would be given the broad outlines of the new policy, the method of operation, and the results expected. This basic education would be designed to encourage justifiable confidence in the new policy and to instill in the general population the broad principles on which resistance in times of crisis would be based.

More specialized training would be required for particular occupational groups and for those wishing to participate in more advanced aspects of the defense policy. The specific forms of training would vary, and the levels would range from that required by local defense workers to specialist education, which could be offered by civilian defense counterparts of West Point. Careful consideration would be needed to determine the

---

[77] For a brief discussion of preparations, see Sharp, "Deterrence and liberation by civilian defence," in Roberts, et al., op. cit., pp. 48-49. For the best and most thorough discussion to date, see Theodor Ebert, "Organizational Preparations for Nonviolent Civilian Defence." Paper prepared for the Civilian Defence Study Conference, Sept. 1964. A revised version of this paper will appear in "The Strategy of Civilian Defence," ed. Adam Roberts, to be published by Faber & Faber, London, in late 1966.

most desirable and effective means of such educational preparations and organizational structures for those actively involved in preparation and training programs.

Specialists in civilian defense could play an important role in initiating resistance, especially at the beginning of an occupation or a coup, and could in specific situations serve as special cadres for particularly dangerous tasks. They could not and should not be depended on to carry out the resistance on behalf of the general population. Responsibility for the bulk of defense measures should be assumed by the citizenry. The specialists' role should be primarily that of assisting in training and in launching the initial resistance. It may be highly desirable to keep some specialists in reserve to guide the later stages of the resistance. In general, the leaders will be among the first imprisoned or otherwise dealt with by the usurper; thus, the population will need to have the capability to continue civilian defense measures on its own initiative.

None of this should be interpreted as implying that preparations for civilian defense should consist only of central instructions carried out at the base of the pyramid. An effective strategy of civilian defense would require an analysis of the potentialities of particular factors—means of transportation, government departments, schools, and so forth—to identify the specific points at which selective non-cooperation might have a maximum impact in disrupting the operation of the whole institution or system. This is simply illustrative of the interplay that would be needed between the group largely responsible for formulating various general strategies of defense and those carrying out measures on the local level. The specific organization of a contact system or an underground would probably have to wait until after the launching of the invasion or coup; otherwise it might be much easier for the opponent to know the exact personnel and structure of the resistance system.

Civilian defense "war games" and defense maneuvers, as part of the preparations, have been proposed by Theodor Ebert.[78] Such war games would offer the specialists a chance to examine the viability of proposed alternative strategies and tactics for dealing with various types of threats. Maneuvers,

---

[78] Ibid.; see also Ebert, "Freedom on the Offensive." A background paper of the Civilian Defence Study Conference. Duplicated.

ranging from ones to be held in local residential areas or factories to ones in cities, regions, and even the whole country, could be useful means by which the population would learn in a small way something of the practical application of the civilian defense principles. Such exercises might help to avoid the uncertainty and bewilderment often experienced by the population in times of invasion or coups d'état, and thereby facilitate the launching of the resistance with the maximum of resolution and unity.

Preparations for civilian defense should also include continued efforts to improve the society and system. In the last analysis, the more worthy the society is of defense, the better that defense will be. Alienated or unjustly treated sections of the population can be a serious threat to success. Since diffusion of power and responsibility is important in the conduct of civilian defense, reforms designed to give such groups a sense of participation in the community and to eradicate injustices could be a contribution by increasing both the degree of democracy and the defense potential.[79]

Technical preparations are also necessary for civilian defense. It would be most desirable, for example, to provide, in advance, provisions and equipment that would lessen difficulties of communication with the population after the enemy has occupied key centers and seized established newspapers, radio stations, and other mass media. Printing and duplicating equipment for underground newspapers and resistance leaflets and broadcasting equipment could be distributed in advance. Thus, if large stocks were discovered and seized, considerable supplies would still be available to counter the enemy's propaganda and to disseminate instructions for resistance. Advance arrangements might often be possible for locating such broadcasting stations or printing plants in the territory of a friendly neighboring country as part of a civilian defense mutual aid agreement. Since an enemy might seek to force submission by starving the population, and since certain resistance methods (such as a general strike) would disrupt the distribution of

---

[79] This important field requires more extensive consideration and investigation than is possible in this article. For an excellent discussion, see April Carter, "Advance Preparations for a Civilian Defence Policy: Political and Economic Problems." Paper prepared for the Civilian Defence Study Conference. A revised version of this paper will appear in "The Strategy of Civilian Defence," op. cit.

food, emergency supplies of food should be stored locally. Alternative means of providing fuel and water during emergencies could also be explored. In particular types of crises, plans might be considered for the dispersal of major sections of the population from large cities to rural areas where control would be more difficult to exercise.

At this point, it is hard to say what would be the best governmental arrangements for the preparation and organization of a civilian defense policy. A Department of Civilian Defense might be set up to provide leadership and coordination. Various types of legislation concerning the adoption and implementation of civilian defense, the responsibility of the citizens, and so forth, would probably be necessary.[80]

Overthrowing the Opponent

The strategists and other experts in or associated with this Department of Civilian Defense would have prime responsibility for considering a variety of possible strategies and tactics for dealing with all conceivable forms that usurpation might take. The strategy most appropriate to a given situation would be determined in a large degree by the nature of the enemy and his objectives. All possible present and future threats and aims, therefore, would require careful advanced study, carried out together with a consideration of various strategies for dealing with each threat. While anticipation of and preparation for all eventualities should be made, the exact course of events is extremely difficult to predict. Provisions would also have to be made to ensure the flexibility and capacity for innovation to meet unexpected situations.

The initial stages of an attempted usurpation will be crucial in setting the mood and pattern of behavior to be developed in later periods. The attitude of the population to the invasion or coup is crucial. Traditionally, occupation following the defeat of military forces has been accompanied by feelings of dismay, confusion, and hopelessness. The defense capacity has been exhausted to no avail, and the population

---

[80] This has been suggested both by Ebert, "Organizational Preparations for Nonviolent Civilian Defence," op. cit.; and by Lars Porsholt, "How to Meet Measures of the Occupying Power Against the Civil Resistance." Paper prepared for the Civilian Defence Study Conference.

is left to fend for itself. This situation contributes significantly to the psychological condition that Hitler prescribed as necessary for successful occupation rule: the people of the occupied territories must admit defeat and recognize the occupation regime as their conqueror and master. Under a civilian defense policy, a radically different situation would exist. The country and the defense capacity would not have been defeated. The combat strength would not yet have been tested in struggle. The citizenry would have been so trained and prepared that it would not feel dismayed or confused. It would be understood that the physical distribution of soldiers and functionaries throughout the country did not constitute defeat but instead was the initial stage of a longer struggle at close range. This admittedly would be difficult, but the civilian defenders would hold advantages. Setbacks and defeats might occur; they would lead, however, not to acceptance of the usurpation but to a period of building strength and regrouping of forces under a different strategy in preparation for greater success in future campaigns. There are no white flags of surrender in civilian defense.

Although civilian defense cannot defend the geographic borders, this does not mean that nothing can be done at this initial stage. The deployment of troops can be delayed by obstructionist activities at the docks if major troop shipments came by sea, by refusal to operate the railroads, or by blocking highways with thousands of abandoned automobiles. Such acts will also make clear to the individual soldiers that any propaganda concerning the population's desire for protection against a threatening third power is not true. Other more symbolic actions with primarily a psychological intent can be undertaken to establish an attitude of resistance and defiance as early as possible. This will serve a dual purpose: (*a*) to give notice to the usurping regime, its functionaries, and its troops that the attempt to seize control and occupy the country will be firmly resisted; and (*b*) to influence the morale and behavior of the general population so that no inactive period will exist during which submission and collaboration can spread because of the absence of articulate opposition.

It will be important, as has been previously indicated, to make special efforts to communicate with the usurper's ordinary troops. They should be informed that there will be resistance. But, to minimize future suffering and increase the chances of victory, they must be helped to understand that, despite what they may have been told, the resistance will be a special type, directed against the attempt to seize control but without threatening harm to the individual soldiers. If this can be communicated, the soldiers may be more likely to help the resisting population in small ways, less likely to carry out brutalities or to conduct repression efficiently, and more likely to mutiny at a crisis point than if they expected at any moment to become targets for snipers or plastic bombs. Radio, leaflets, and personal conversations (preferably in the soldiers' own language) may be used for this purpose. Certain types of demonstrations may conceivably be held at the border or at other points where troops may enter, but their limited role will have to be recognized. Other initial actions may include the wearing of black by the whole population as a symbol of disapproval, a stay-at-home for one or more days, a general strike for a limited predetermined period, and the defiance of curfews with multitudes of the people flooding the streets and behaving in a friendly fashion to the individual soldiers, asking them to visit their homes, and urging them not to believe the propaganda they may have heard.

Strategies of Civilian Struggle

Depending on the assessment of the opponent and the situation, a well-prepared population might possibly undertake a hard campaign of comprehensive non-cooperation intended to force quick defeat of the attempt to seize power. The general strike would be a key method for this kind of campaign, which has been called a "nonviolent *blitzkrieg*."[81]

    A program of total non-cooperation with the enemy would doubtless be the most effective strategy, if the population could maintain such non-cooperation with something approaching unanimity even in the face of severe repression, and if it were able to organize and continue life itself during the struggle. The difficulties of fulfilling these conditions may mean that sometimes such extensive non-cooperation will not be attempted. In any case, it could be effectively practiced only for

[81] Ebert, "Freedom on the Offensive," op. cit.

limited time periods. This strategy, therefore, might be reserved for initial attempts at quick defeat of usurpation, applied as short, extra severe resistance at particular points in the course of a long struggle, or used toward the end of a prolonged struggle to bring it to a swift, successful close.

It should already be obvious, even in this very sketchy discussion, that there are a variety of possible strategies that might be applied in civilian defense.[82] If one strategy is inappropriate in a given circumstance or after use has not proved effective, other possible strategies exist, and within each one there is considerable room for variation. Transitions from one strategy to another and from one phase of the conflict to the next are very important; flexibility without a sense of failure and realistic assessments of the state of the struggle without an abandonment of confidence and loss of initiative are crucial though difficult to achieve. If a "nonviolent *blitzkrieg*," or total resistance, has been attempted and has not produced victory after a reasonable time, a transition to more selective resistance over a longer time schedule would be necessary.

Directly after the stage of initial symbolic resistance or after a period of general strike or total resistance, the strategy of selective resistance could be applied. Such a strategy provides for the concentration of resistance at specific points crucial to the usurper's control, or at those particularly important for the maintenance of the principles and way of life of the country. There are several potential advantages of this strategy. First, it may involve an economic use of combat strength. For a certain period of time the main brunt of the struggle may be borne by a particular section of the population, such as an occupational group, and the rest of the population, though involved in various ways, does not constantly have to be the primary target of attack. Other sections of the population may take the lead later and assume the brunt of the struggle. Second, as tyrannical, and particularly totalitarian, regimes seek to achieve and maintain control by the stage-by-stage destruction of independent groups and institutions and the atomization of the population, selective resistance can be focused on defense of the independence of particular groups and institutions, such as trade unions, schools,

---

[82] See Roberts, "Alternative Strategies in Facing Invasion." Paper prepared for the Civilian Defence Study Conference.

and churches, that may be subject to attack at any given point. Successful resistance at these points helps both to retain and to develop the society's capacity for future resistance and its qualities of freedom. Third, selective resistance in either defensive or offensive forms may be directed at those points which symbolize important issues, for example, the freedoms of speech, religion, and assembly, in the battle of ideas between the two systems. In addition to being simply the battlegrounds over which the contest of forces takes place, they are, by the very selection and formulation of the specific issues, important factors in the ideological and psychological aspects of the struggle. "Resistance at the right point can help to communicate to an enemy, to the civilian population, and to third parties, exactly what is being fought for, and what is being proposed."[83] Last, selective resistance applied to transportation, industry, and other aspects of the economic system can be very effective in thwarting the enemy's general control and specific economic objectives. Careful selection of the issues and points of resistance may go a long way to maximize the power of the civilian defenders and to achieve successes against the usurping regime.

As selective resistance is likely to be more frequently applied than total resistance, it would be crucial to decide well ahead of time on the types of issues to which resistance must be offered and on the points at which ground must never be given even for tactical reasons, whatever the price. These would generally be points of overwhelming ideological significance or points that, if granted, would ensure the enemy control of the society.[84] Citizens as a whole and each occupational group should be familiar with these preselected points, thereby facilitating response to particular resistance instructions or ensuring resistance at such points even if the resistance organization were destroyed. Within selective resistance, the strategy may be developed in various specific ways to counter most adequately the opponent's objectives and to accord with particular social and political conditions.

It is impossible here to suggest detailed courses of resistance in particular conflict situations or to explore all the kinds of strategic considerations and alternatives that lie within

---
[83] Ibid.
[84] See Porsholt, op. cit.

the field of strategy in civilian defense. No two situations are ever exactly alike. Careful investigation and planning are required to determine for a particular conflict what are the more promising strategies and tactics. The consideration of general principles of civilian defense strategy is a vast task, which for several reasons may be more comprehensive and difficult than military strategy. The whole population and all the institutions of the society potentially are directly involved in the struggle itself. In a nonviolent war, the battleground is not limited to geographic front lines or foreign targets. It includes the whole country, the international theater of operations in which non-military support is sought against the invader, and the invader's own homeland where domestic opposition to the invader's regime and its aggression should be encouraged.[85]

As long as the citizens remain firm and refuse to cooperate and obey, they hold the real power. "For the tyrant has the power to inflict only that which we lack the strength to resist."[86] A dictator is no less dependent upon the sources of power granted to him by the subjects than any other ruler. If these sources of his power can be withheld by the non-cooperation and disobedience of the population, he, too, will be unable to maintain himself as a ruler.

The problem of defense, therefore, is the problem of how to act by means that undermine and finally dissolve the usurper's power to maintain his usurpation. There are admittedly a multitude of difficult questions involved in such an attempt. In addition to those already suggested, four merit special mention. (1) What is the most desirable and effective approach to the opponent's troops and functionaries in order to encourage disaffection, obtain cooperation, and perhaps finally induce a mutiny? Two diametrically opposite approaches have been suggested: social boycott, and individual fraternization combined with political non-cooperation. (2) With varying degrees of individual commitment and involvement, how can the maximum level of citizenry participation be obtained? (Total participation is not necessary for success.) Since certain occupational groups

---
[85] For the most comprehensive discussion to date of these various theaters and alternative and supplementary strategies, see Ebert, "The Strategy of Civilian Nonviolent War." Paper prepared for the Civilian Defence Study Conference.
[86] Krishnalal Shridharani, *War Without Violence* (New York: Harcourt, Brace and Co., 1939), p. 305.

may be especially vulnerable and simultaneously hold extremely important positions, their behavior requires special attention. (3) In the face of repression and brutalities, how can the defenders' capacity to persist be strengthened to the utmost? Military might has been demonstrated to be incapable of imposing a regime on a population firmly determined not to accept it.[87] It is necessary, however, to study the conditions under which this is possible and the influence on these of various types of repression, including psychological warfare, drugs, *agents provocateurs,* seizure of hostages, selective acts of terror, and vast physical destruction. (4) Can civilian defense be combined with military defense or at least with sabotage? Although this requires careful investigation and research, there is one important argument against the attempt to do so. The mechanisms of change in the two techniques of struggle are quite different from those in non-violent action; the latter is seriously weakened by violence from the resisters. A combination of these may destroy the effectiveness of the civilian defense actions and the operation of the political *jiu jitsu* process in which the opponent's violence, in the face of the defenders' nonviolence, rebounds against his power position. This suggests that in the absence of greater knowledge it is unwise to make a hasty decision to combine them.

Possibility of Defeat

A defense of political freedom such as that proposed here would never be easy. There would be suffering, tragedies, and setbacks as well as dignity, heroism, and successes. There would be no certainty of easy or short-term victories; there would be no way of guaranteeing that such a struggle would inevitably lead to success even in the space of a few years. No technique of struggle can guarantee clear victory in every instance in which it is applied. There are a multitude of factors involved in a civilian defense struggle. If the qualities and conditions necessary for the successful operation of the mechanisms of nonviolent action are not present to a sufficient degree, victory cannot follow. Many of these factors, however, are directly

---

[87] Although fear of nuclear attack is a strong motive for launching one, according to some military men, the odds in favor of the use of nuclear weapons against a country using civilian defense are extremely low.

and indirectly controllable by the nonviolent actionists. This is one reason why research, planning, preparations, and training are so important for civilian defense and significantly increase the chances of victory.

In considering the possibility of failure or of only very limited success, two factors need to be kept in mind. First, even failure after an heroic struggle by civilian defense is preferable to any outcome of a major nuclear war. At worst, it would mean a long, difficult, and painful existence under severe tyranny, but life would still remain, and with life the hope for eventual freedom. Emphatically, this is not a brief for the "better red than dead" type of slogan. It is not the abandonment of strength but the reverse. Nonviolent action is not a course for cowards. It requires the ability to sustain the battle whatever the price in suffering, yet would, in any case, allow a future for mankind. Second, in this type of struggle, the failure to achieve total victory does not mean total defeat. Even if the population of the occupied country should lack the capacity to drive out the invader, it could have the strength to maintain a considerable degree of autonomy for the country and a large degree of independence for the social and political institutions upon which the country's capacity for freedom largely depends. The defense struggle could also exert pressures to lessen the brutality and rigidity of sections of the invader's own government and population.

There are many reasons for believing that an adequately prepared civilian defense policy would make it possible to overthrow an occupation or a coup and restore political freedom. If a country makes the maximum possible effort to fulfill the requirements of a civilian defense policy, there are grounds for thinking that, under present international and technological conditions, civilian defense offers a much greater chance of success than does military defense.

The Tyrant Faces Impotence

A number of the responses that may be made to create a political ambush and to deny the invader his political and economic objectives have been indicated. It may be worthwhile, however, to briefly recapitulate these possible activities.

At the initial stage, he may find that the railways, airlines, buses, and even private vehicles are not available to transport his soldiers and officials because of the refusal of transport workers and transportation experts to cooperate. He may discover the removal of key parts from the equipment or the absence of necessary fuel. He may meet a blanket refusal on the part of the existing government bureaucracy and civil servants to take any action, or they may continue to carry out the old policies, ignore his orders, and disrupt the implementation of new policies. The existing police, instead of helping to make arrests, carry over some resemblance of order, and encourage obedience to the new regime, may blatantly go on strike, disappear under new identities, or at least warn the resistance movement and population of impending arrests. Furthermore, the police may also selectively refuse to carry out orders or carry them out with such inefficiency that they are of little use.

The invader's parades of troops throughout the cities may be met with empty streets and shuttered windows, and his public receptions boycotted. Efforts may be made to undermine the loyalty of his individual soldiers and functionaries. They may be invited to dinners and parties with individuals and families and tactfully explained the aims and nonviolent means of the resistance. Attempts to utilize the economic system may be met with limited general strikes, slow-downs, the refusal of assistance or disappearance of indispensable experts, and the selective use of various types of strikes at key points in industries, transportation, and the supply of raw materials. The resistance may be publicized through prearranged channels throughout the world, including the invader's homeland.

At the intermediary stage, the enemy may gradually try to gain control of the various social institutions, either because their independence contributes significantly to the population's capacity to resist or because control is required by the tyrant's ideology or political program. By its very nature, totalitarianism must seek to bring all major social institutions under the control of the state, as a part of the atomization of the population and the regimentation of the society. If this is achieved, the future capacity for resistance will be largely destroyed for a long period. Thus, because of democratic principles and future combat capacity, civilian defense will firmly resist any efforts to control the society's institutions.

The attempt to use the legal court system to bolster the authority of the new regime or to enforce its orders would be met by refusals to recognize the usurping regime as legal and constitutional, and often by refusal of judges to continue to operate the courts under existing political conditions. The attempt to bring the school system under state control by dissolving independent teachers' organizations and school boards, by setting up substitute politically controlled bodies, and by introducing propaganda into the curriculum would be confronted with a refusal to recognize the dissolution of the former organizations, a refusal to include anti-democratic propaganda in the curriculum, explanations to the pupils of the issues at stake in the defense struggle, and perhaps the closing of school buildings and the holding of free private classes in the children's homes. Efforts to destroy the independence of trade unions and to establish politically controlled puppet organizations would be met by refusal to attend meetings of or pay dues to the new bodies, by persistence in recognizing only the earlier organizations, and by engaging in a series of disruptive strikes and boycotts that would cause grave difficulties for the usurping regime. Innumerable ways can be envisaged by which attempts to take over other institutions and occupational groups (the churches, management, newspapers, radio, farmers, electricians) could be opposed by similar non-cooperation and defiance. There are historical precedents for all of these types of resistance. Even without advance preparations they have been highly effective in important cases. With careful advance instruction, training, and other types of preparations, there is every reason to believe that the effectiveness of such non-cooperation could be greatly increased.

The failure to bring the occupied country to heel and to destroy social institutions would indicate that the society's capacity to resist had been sustained; its skill in doing so may have increased with combat experience. Moreover, the psychological climate created would tend to produce or increase a miasma of uncertainty and dissent within the usurper's regime, in his country, and among his soldiers and functionaries. International pressures may also have been encouraged by the course of events and the defender's evident will to resist. The usurper may find that he faces not only the opposition of world public opinion but serious diplomatic pressures and economic embargoes on important raw materials and manufactured products. In such a situation, repression feeds resistance—the greater the repression, the stronger the resistance. The simple numerical multiplication of non-cooperating and disobedient subjects may thus defeat the would-be tyrant and bring about a restoration of liberty, enhanced with new meaning, vitality, and durability. The initial apparent success of the invasion or early stages of the coup is revealed as a mirage without lasting political reality. The real conquest is effected by the determined civilian defenders of freedom.

The Policy and the World Community

If it is at least conceivable that a well-developed and well-prepared civilian defense policy can serve as a deterrent to international aggression and internal coups d'état, and can defeat attempted occupations and seizures of power, what bearing does this have on the abolition of war? What contributions, both indirect and direct, can civilian defense make to this goal? Where will the adoption of such a policy meet the greatest resistance? Can civilian defense be initiated in one or only a few countries and with what effect? How can civilian defense, which is designed to be a viable alternative defense policy in a world where most countries still maintain military capacity and where international aggression is still possible, play a major role in the abolition of war on a global scale?

No defense policy—military or civilian—operates in a vacuum. It influences and is influenced by the country's foreign policy. It has been effectively argued that the nature and requirements of military defense today impose limitations on the country's other international policies in ways that reduce the country's contributions to world peace. Transarmament to civilian defense is likely to remove these limitations and facilitate the choice and implementation of policies in closer harmony with the country's political principles and with conditions conducive to world peace. Civilian defense is not a panacea that would eliminate the need for other peace policies but, on the contrary, would serve as a stimulus. The foreign policy of a country with a civilian defense policy would thus be far from isolationist. It would continue to participate in a variety of international activities and organizations and deal with the causes of conflict as well as actual outbreaks of violence.

Civilian defense has a potentially significant contribution to make to the reduction of international tensions. It virtually eliminates the fear and distrust that a country's military defense preparations often arouse because they can also be used for aggression. Since civilian defense has no such capacity, many of the fears created by the build-up of military defense capacity are removed. Confirmation of the peaceful intentions of a country is in itself a contribution to international peace.

Civilian defense is also intended to contribute directly to the elimination of war from international society. It provides a political equivalent to military defense that is currently available and not dependent, as universal disarmament or world government is, upon a prior transformation of human society. Both the deterrent effects of civilian defense and its appeal to countries that still rely on a traditional military establishment would depend, in part, on the ability to make clear that the policy is neither a smokescreen to hide secret weapons nor an admission of helplessness. The policy would, therefore, need to be accompanied by a thorough international information program concerning the nature and potential of the policy.

There would inevitably be strongholds of resistance. Democratic powers with large military establishments are unlikely, and probably unable, to eliminate these in a short span of time. They might, however, add a civilian defense component, if its effectiveness could be convincingly demonstrated. They might increasingly rely on this component until the substitution is completed. Dictatorial regimes and unstable governments probably would cling hardest to military capacity for both domestic and international purposes. Civilian defense cannot be used to "liberate" another country or to provide the foundations of national solidarity and stability where these are lacking. In the case of a dictatorship, however, two possibilities of exerting influence exist. First, where the dictatorship has been motivated partly by fear of foreign attack, the adoption of civilian defense by its erstwhile potential aggressors could lessen this fear and permit some relaxation. Second, the absence of military threats from countries with civilian defense policies removes, as far as these countries are concerned, the opportunity to use such threats to keep the population submissive. Moreover, the example set by countries employing civilian defense policies might inspire the population to press for greater freedom. If the reduction of tyranny is encouraged as a byproduct of civilian defense in a number of countries, this is potentially an important contribution to international peace as well as to political freedom. Similarly, unstable governments might find aspects of civilian defense that would help them establish a sense of national loyalty among the people.

The adoption by communist countries of civilian defense would be a radical development, but this is not inconceivable. It would depend, to a great extent, on the seriousness with which early socialist ideals and ultimate socialist goals are taken by their present and future leadership. Early socialist doctrine was strongly anti-militarist. The political intention was to abolish capitalism and tyranny as well as the state itself.

After the Bolshevik seizure of power in Russia, there was some consideration of the type of defense appropriate for a socialist country. Military defense of the traditional type was settled upon to deal with actual or potential foreign intervention and invasion. This not only led to a defense policy in the Soviet Union virtually indistinguishable from capitalist countries, but, according to Stalin himself, also influenced the whole development of party and government. Stalin used arguments of national security against pleas for freedom of discussion within the Communist Party: Russia was "surrounded by the wolves of imperialism; and to discuss all important matters in 20,000 party cells would mean to lay all one's cards before the enemy."[88] He also maintained that the needs of military security were among other reasons why a workers' democracy was the "impossible." At one point, Stalin explained the divergence of the Soviet regime from the 1917 ideal—"the attainment of which [is] still far off." By this prescription,

---

[88] As quoted in I. Deutscher, *Stalin: A Political Biography* (London: Oxford Univ. Press, 1949), p. 258.

what is needed to free the state from bureaucratic elements ... is a high degree of civilization in the people, a completely secure, peaceful condition all round, so that we should not need large military cadres ... which put their imprint on the other governmental institutions....[89]

It would be possible to interpret a change to civilian defense as justified by socialist ideology. Past military defense could be explained as an unfortunate historical necessity beyond which it is now possible to move. It could also be attributed partially to the distortions of socialism encouraged by Trotsky, who organized the Red Army, and Stalin. Civilian defense could be interpreted as more in harmony with earlier socialist doctrine that placed confidence in the power of the workers. In one of Lenin's last speeches, for example, he reminded his followers of times in history when the civilization of the conquerors was inferior to that of the conquered. In these situations, according to Lenin, the latter was able to impose its civilization on the former.[90]

A change to civilian defense in communist countries is thus not inconceivable at some future time. Such a change would hinge on the best possible view of Soviet society and intentions. It would require genuine popular support for the system, absence of aggressive military intentions, and a willingness to de-Stalinize to the extent of devolving and diffusing power throughout the society to a hitherto unachieved degree.

Although one can assume that initially only a few countries would adopt a civilian defense policy, it is still impossible to outline with any precision or certainty the effect this would have on the course of international relations. The decision and transarmament would have to depend on the state of knowledge and understanding, the adequacy of the strategic planning, the quality and extent of preparations, the type of citizen training, and the determination, skill, and heroism with which the policy was implemented. All of these factors will be highly influential in determining whether or not the particular application of civilian defense utilizes and demonstrates the maximum potential of the policy. A visual demonstration of a carefully prepared civilian defense successfully defeating a seizure of

---
[89] As quoted in ibid., p. 263; see also ibid., pp. 226 and 285.
[90] See ibid., p. 359.

power or occupation might make a significant contribution toward the adoption of the policy by other countries. If, however, early applications of this policy were poorly prepared and conducted, the result could be to discredit the whole idea.

If the initial developments and applications in civilian defense were to show sufficient promise and effectiveness, it is quite possible that more and more countries interested in both adequate defense and international peace would investigate, consider, and finally transarm to the new policy. This type of development could be directly encouraged by the countries that had already investigated and adopted civilian defense. Countries with civilian defense policies could help each other in various ways: by such measures as civilian defense mutual assistance pacts under which they could cooperate in a detailed sharing of knowledge and experience in various aspects of civilian defense; by providing certain types of aid (food and other supplies, financial help, diplomatic and economic pressures against the aggressor, a haven for escapees, safe printing and broadcasting facilities) at times of attempted usurpation; by cooperative efforts to provide interested countries with information on civilian defense; and by various combined activities to reduce the pressures and temptations for aggression and coups.

As contrasted with military data, a sharing of results of research, investigation, planning, preparations, and training programs would not normally endanger future combat effectiveness. The expansion and accumulation of such knowledge added to increased experience could lead, first, to greater general confidence in the viability of civilian defense and, eventually, to a significant acceleration in the rate at which countries transarmed to civilian defense. This development would be of major importance in a step-by-step removal of war from the international arena.

It is quite conceivable that some countries might never abandon military capacity. That would not, however, be a reason for abandoning civilian defense, but rather for expanding it and improving its effectiveness. The need for defense capacity against internal and external would-be dictators will long be present. The state of knowledge of this technique and policy, however, is still extremely primitive. It will be necessary, as has been stated, to analyze the nature of totalitarian regimes, with particular reference to their sources of power and means of repression and their inherent weaknesses. How can these weaknesses be accentuated by nonviolent means to induce the regimes either to liberalize themselves or to disintegrate? Under what conditions can the disaffection and mutiny of their troops be successfully fomented?

A study of past occupations by totalitarian and non-totalitarian regimes and of violent and nonviolent resistance movements will have to be made. What are the theories, mechanisms, and dynamics of nonviolent action, including the variant strategies and requirements for success? What is the relationship of nonviolent action and civilian defense to various social and political systems; which are most compatible with the policy and which most alien to it? What problems are encountered in preparing and training for civilian defense, in operating a resistance movement, and in maintaining an underground organization under conditions of severe repression and totalitarian controls? What is the effect of combining civilian defense with sabotage and military defense? What are the foreign policy requirements for an optimal civilian defense policy?

Civilian defense is designed to operate in a world of conflict, aggression, and broken promises; a world of distrust and suspicion; a world in which not only tyrants but political mad-men sometimes occupy positions of power and honor; and a world in which, even if all military weapons systems are destroyed, they can be built again. Civilian defense, therefore, has not been developed as a policy for a future Utopia. It is based on the premise that defense today, if it is to be real and not simply destructive, must be self-defense. Lasting and genuine freedom depends upon internal strength and the capacity of the citizens to defend it against all usurpers. Civilian defense may ultimately prove to be a major contribution to the solution of the problem of war. Upon investigation it may also prove to be a dead end. However, considering the seriousness of our need, no possible solution for which a reasonable case can be made ought to go uninvestigated. An answer to so grave a problem as this should be based on an accurate perception of the real and tragic world in which we must live.

Such an answer has to be formulated in concrete and practical terms to meet the realities of that world. It will also have to be a solution susceptible of application by ordinary men and women, who are capable, it must be remembered, of extraordinary qualities. The answer cannot be a doctrine or a system that is simply accepted in order to solve the problem once and for all. Measures for abolishing war will have to operate stage-by-stage and be applied, tested, improved, and reapplied as one seeks to move from one situation to the creation of another, which in turn makes possible a new move and a new situation, and on and on until war is removed from human society.

JX1907.Am35

~~272.4~~
~~SHA~~

Sharp, Gene
The Political Equivalent of
War -- Civilian Defense

DATE DUE			

KANSAS SCHOOL OF RELIGION
UNIVERSITY OF KANSAS
1300 OREAD AVENUE
LAWRENCE, KANSAS 66044

DEMCO